The Drive of Business:

Strategies for Creating Business Angles

First published in 2016
by Hughes Consulting Limited
Registered number 05067369
www.hughesconsult.co.uk

A CIP record for this book is available from the British Library.

ISBN 978-0-9955271-0-2

To my family

About the author

Robert David Hughes is a strategic management consultant. He is a Certified Management Consultant (Member of the Institute of Consulting), Chartered Engineer (Member of the Institution of Engineering and Technology), Chartered Information Technology Professional (Member of the British Computer Society) and Chartered Manager (Member of the Chartered Management Institute), and holds a Doctorate in Business Administration. He has published a number of papers on a range of topics and contributed as a visiting lecturer to post graduate degree programmes.

He is principal of the United Kingdom and New Zealand based management consulting firm Hughes Consulting Limited. Prior to his current role, he was a partner in the international business advisory firm KPMG. Clients of Hughes Consulting are significant organisations located in New Zealand, Australia and the United Kingdom.

His key skill set is leading organisational change: developing and exploiting core competencies; repositioning in the market - especially multi-sided markets (markets characterised by strong positive cross-group effects such as the postal network of receivers and senders) and network industries; and taking advantage of the digital economy (in particular exploiting information and telecommunications technology, and large-scale data processing systems).

A hallmark of his working relationship with clients is to provide thought leadership on a vision for the future, mentoring on the leadership required to implement strategic change, and transferring this knowledge to the client organisation. He most commonly works as counsel to C-suite executives.

In addition to establishing Hughes Consulting, he has founded: a software business that provides technology to provision business processes as software-as-a-service (SaaS) applications; a software business that provides tools to support the administrative processes required to discharge legal obligations; and an agri-business.

Contents

Introduction

Scope

Conceiving new business opportunities comes easily to many people. For some the opportunity is perceived with great clarity and held with passion. It is quite another matter to take the idea of an opportunity and turn it into a fully formed business model, particularly one that has some prospect of making a profit. Here, the creative challenge of building a successful business can be on a par with fashioning a great work of art. There is a fine line between entrepreneurial insight and self-delusion when it comes to working out how to go about exploiting a perceived opportunity profitably. Too frequently businesspeople pay little attention to market context and activity type to be employed. This is surprising because activity type, which refers to the operational capabilities to be used in the production process, is intrinsically linked to market context.

Activity type aligns business objectives and constraints with conditions found in the market. To give an example, there is a business opportunity in carbon farming to grow trees with large mass and long lifespan which sequestrate large volumes of carbon from the atmosphere enabling the sale of carbon credits. There is a range of ways that could be used to turn this idea into a business. One way is through direct ownership of forestry assets - a self-contained forestry business could be established with capabilities in a nursery to grow seedlings, forest management, silviculture, carbon accounting, and sale of carbon credits. This solution involves employing people and investing in land, trees, buildings, plant, and equipment. It is a comparatively capital intensive business model. An alternative way requiring less capital, is to invest only in the land and trees, and purchase the various services needed on contract. A third way, in addition to contracting for forestry services, is to dispense with the upfront costs of owning the land by leasing it from the owner. Each of these alternatives involves a different activity type, with the differences being reflected in the capital investment required, timing of that investment, risk of the venture, and the expected return. Indeed, where the first way is the traditional concept of a business enterprise, the third alternative is more like a financial instrument.

These three ways of participating in carbon farming involve a long wait for a return, with positive cash flows commencing between 10 and 20 years after planting the trees. For many, waiting this long, even given the environmental benefits, is just not feasible, but there are other fee-earning activities that may be more appropriate. These include promoting investment in carbon farming, managing forestry ventures owned by others; genetics, nursery, silviculture, pest management, recreation, measurement, accounting and carbon trading. All these businesses share in the value added from carbon farming but differ in their capabilities, capital requirement, cash flow profile over time, return expectations and risk.

The topic of this book is how to transform a perceived business opportunity into an actual business proposition through the choice of the activity type to be adopted. Perceived business opportunities stem from expectations to profit from enterprise and speculation. Quite different types of activities can be employed to form a business angle through which to exploit the opportunity. Business angles can be crafted with different capital requirements and capacities to generate return and risk. This topic is important because it helps businesspeople better understand the ways in which business angles are formulated to exploit a perceived business opportunity within the context of the market, and subsequently succeed.

A wide range of activity types are used in the market in the pursuit of profit from a business opportunity. The choice of activity type is intertwined with decisions concerning the boundary of the business's capabilities within a value network. But this is not simply a choice between one or two well-established alternatives for organising the production technologies. Whilst, at any point in time there are a few dominant activity types in any sector, it would be short-sighted to conclude that this points to some universal static set of successful activity types. One reason for this is that the apparent stability of markets that results from the success of certain business angles, in fact changes the market, and creates other opportunities, which can then be exploited using quite different activity types.

This book also explores the ability to earn profits from different positions and ways of participating in a value network, and the consequences for the composition of a business's capabilities. Organisational structure, the other component in the design of the business model, and the interrelationship between knowhow, systems and processes, and organisational structure are not explored in this book.

Origin of the ideas

There are many inspirations behind the ideas set out in this book. There are, however, two main strands that are brought together so that activity types can be matched with conditions faced in the market. The first strand is derived from process and systems engineering. Its foundations can be traced back to the early nineteenth century, but it emerged as a distinct discipline in the latter half of the twentieth century. Systems and process engineering view business activities as organisations of capabilities composed of outputs, inputs, information, knowhow, systems and processes, being coordinated in pursuit of an overarching purpose. The second strand draws from economics and focuses on the nature of commercial exchanges, a key element of which is the idea that speculation is a central component of business decisions. This idea has a long pedigree. It is discussed notably by John Maynard Keynes in *The General Theory of Employment, Interest and Money*, published in 1936.

The synthesis of these strands and the other ideas in this book have been shaped by a mix of my hands-on experience as a management consultant, empirical research, and the works and writings of a vast number of researchers and thinkers. My experience has been gained from a career in management consulting spanning more than 30 years, working with significant organisations primarily in New Zealand and the United Kingdom - two markets with very different characteristics. Drawing on these experiences, ideas are illustrated by describing different conditions and situations found in specific business settings. Chapters end with a summary of the key works and writing that have helped me form some of these ideas. Invariably these works and writings form a broad flow of ideas picked up, explored and extended by others. This process of crediting precedents is equivalent to that found in music where later works are acknowledged as being inspired by earlier works. In some cases early sources of inspiration for the later works and writings can be traced, and these too are credited in order to give recognition to the continuity of the flow of ideas over time.

Propositions made

A business's value depends in part on the flexibility with which it can adapt to external factors, such as changes in markets, societal expectations or competing alternatives. This flexibility translates into value through the business strategy and its motivation to change its organisational architecture (at least as far as the organisation's architecture relates to the allocation of authority to decide and take action, control systems, performance evaluation and reward systems).

The book advances four key propositions about the role of activity types in creating feasible business angles. First, at any point in the value network there is a range of quite different activity types available to exploit a business opportunity. Second, the range of alternative feasible business angles is determined by the place in the value network and context in which the business chooses to operate. Third, the choice of activity type is central to the design of the business angle. Fourth, the choice of activity type is influenced by a number of factors including market context, purpose, strategy, extent of market turbulence, as well as business lifecycle and market maturation.

The importance of knowing about markets

Market context covers all aspects of the external environment within which a business operates. It is within context that situations arise from which business opportunities emerge. Methods have been developed for describing business context, nonetheless, its analysis is often problematic to formularise, particularly as it relates to new opportunities with little precedent. Emerging opportunities may be difficult to identify at an early stage. In addition, there is little agreement as to the precise nature of the emergent opportunity, even amongst those most intimately involved in that market. Frequently, it is only with hindsight that matters become clear, and by this stage the opportunity has matured and new opportunities arisen.

Uncertainty applies in all markets in which a business operates. Taking one illustration, the behaviour of market prices is always capable of delivering surprises even, or especially, when it seems that they are highly predictable. An example of this was the consistent increases in real estate prices in the period leading up to the Global Financial Crisis of 2007. People do know, however, that markets are uncertain and full of surprises, even if they do not like it. Uncertainty is the essential ingredient for speculative gains. Without uncertainty, there is no scope for alternative views among different participants in the market, no differences in assessments of current or future value, and therefore no basis for speculation.

Given an uncertain future, businesspeople are on the hunt to discover speculative opportunities and some angle through which to profit from them. The profit comes from picking and investing in products and resources to which the market attaches a higher price than the cost of acquiring them.

To exploit a perceived business opportunity, businesses employ an extensive range of different activity types. Activity types alter the boundaries of the business by determining the allocation of capabilities and risk to parties with the greatest readiness and appetite to take them on. An explanation for this is entrepreneurial alertness, which is a dynamic concept. On the one hand, businesses already in a market seek ways to shape it to their own advantage. These businesses find ways to parlay their resources into new positions in the market. On the other hand, new entrants are alert to perceived conditions that change the position of the incumbents in the market; and market instability is the manifestation of the ebb and flow of perceived opportunities to extract a share of the value added from a value network.

Where there is an expectation that ongoing profit is attainable from change and structural imperfections in the market, then investment will continue in existing businesses and in new entrants. It is also expected that some new entrants, rather than copying the incumbents, will find different activity types to exploit the market opportunity. This is especially the case where the assessed threshold for participating in the opportunity is acceptably low because an activity type is available.

The four key propositions above impact on the choice of activity type in the design of a viable business angle. They are presented as focusing on the business as an enterprise, and this could give the impression that analysis of business opportunities should be undertaken at a high, strategic level. This is incorrect. Businesses should be defined *"from a number of different viewpoints ranging from the overall macroscopic description... to a detailed microscopic analysis of the [information,] physical and chemical processes taking place and the static and dynamic interactions involved."* (quoted from John Parnaby's 1979 article 'Concept of a manufacturing system', reprinted in Systems Behaviour edited by the Open Systems Group with the third edition published by Harper and Row in 1991. Text in brackets added by author).

Importance of knowing about types of activities

The approaches and frameworks set out in this book provide a systematic explanation of how to evaluate and make best use of the resources available, and how to parlay them into new business angles. These matters are fundamental to the creation and continued existence of all businesses. Being able to successfully establish a business venture with a view to exploit an opportunity is at least as important as identifying the opportunity in the first place. Long-term survival depends on competing and thriving by adopting new business angles as market context changes and new opportunities become available.

The frameworks described are relevant to business strategy. Aside from helping to formulate alternative business angles, they help frame the questions that should be considered in the investment decision-making process. A range of alternative activity types is provided, each with different capital, risk and return profiles, so that an appropriate business angle can be crafted to match the businessperson's preferences. The existence of differing preferences means that different activity types may be selected to pursue the same perceived business opportunity.

High levels of creativity are evident in the design and market positioning of many new businesses. Some of these businesses grow to be admired enterprises, while most go unrecognised, and commonly fail. An often overlooked area of creative endeavour is the activity type that is adopted by a business and then modified over time. It is overlooked because activity type is not visible from outside the business. By applying the frameworks described in this book the nuances of the implemented business angle can be appreciated. These frameworks are a lens through which to better understand the business as a vehicle to exploit business opportunities. Determining the activity type is important since it is this that provides the way for a businessperson to utilise the resources available. From this starting point the businessperson crafts capabilities in the form of the business angle, aligned to the characteristics of the markets in which the business is to operate. All parties are brought together through the design of the activity type. As a result, the activity type consists of the operational capabilities for acquiring inputs for transformation, and delivery as outputs of the business.

Activity types are distinguished by the combination of the delivery and acquisition methods employed. Four terms: assemble, assign, aggregate and arbitrage, apply to both the delivery and acquisition methods. This give rise to a matrix of four delivery methods by four acquisition methods resulting in a total of 16 'sentinel' activity types. The 'assemble method' represents the capabilities to transform raw materials into new products. A very wide range of capabilities are covered by this method, including those used in manufacturing, farming and professional services, hospitality and the creative industries. The 'assign method' is associated with the provision of capacity to enable businesses to contract-out part of the risk in producing outputs - be it in the form of warehouse space, contract manufacturing or outsourcing. The 'aggregate method' is distinguished by the use of the law of large numbers or scale-free infrastructure networks whose costs fall because of the power law (these are referred to as scale-free infrastructure networks). The 'arbitrage method' exploits information asymmetries and transaction costs. Examples of this are found in retailing, wholesaling and various forms of broking.

In practice the activity types actually used are hybrids or combinations of more than one of these 16 sentinel types. This framework provides a method to unpick, identify and classify the activities involved.

All methods use information, apply knowledge by employing systems and processes, consume inputs and carry risk. They differ in how these are used, specifically in the sources of economic advantage that can be taken or drawn on. As a generalisation, in a comparative sense the assemble method involves more of everything, including risk, while the arbitrage method can involve less of everything, and the other two methods fall in the range between these two. This is a sweeping statement, because each method can require high levels of skill, capabilities, capital and other resources and involve substantial risk. The adoption of different activity types by businesses changes the shape of the value network. The ability to exploit different ways to use resources, declining cost economies and managing risk create the openings in the markets the business operate in. The interplay between the different combinations of these methods in a value network can also create openings for disrupting a market.

Here you have one of the principal ideas of this book. Central to this thinking is a framework of 16 sentinel activity types embodying core competencies, which, when combined with the perceived market opportunity, create an angle through which to participate in a value network. Businesses use these activity types, variants and combinations of them to: explore and evaluate ways to exploit perceived opportunities, and accommodate business objectives and constraints; give operational effect to a business angle; reposition in a market; respond to changing market conditions; and parlay core competencies into new angles.

Ways in which business opportunities can arise

There is a broad range of settings in which business opportunities arise. These settings include:

- Time and ignorance changing the context of the market and the proportion of speculation.
- Market context changing over the lifecycle of the opportunity.
- A business operating simultaneously in a number of different markets, each of which contributes new opportunities for profit.
- Businesspeople having different capital, risk and return profiles.
- That there are different orders of market play.
- Scarce resources being parlayed along different development paths.
- Removal of friction between transacting businesses opening up new opportunities in a value network.
- Markets being turbulent.
- The lifecycle of an opportunity and the lifespan of business being different.
- There being different market positioning strategies available for businesses to compete in markets.

There are strategies available to realise value by pursuing a business angle in each of these settings, and these are described in the book.

Approach taken to present these ideas

The key concepts about creating business angles are set out in the following four chapters. These concepts are:

- Business opportunities are perceived sources of profit. Businesspeople pursue market opportunities as potential sources of profit, and in doing so speculate that the opportunity will meet their expected level of profit. The ramifications of uncertainty and investment in capacity to respond are explored.
- Businesses share in the available value added from several markets. A business operates simultaneously in a number of different markets. Each of these markets contributes opportunities for profit. How a share of the available value added is captured from each market is discussed.

- The entire value network matters. The characteristics of the entire value network and market context shape a business opportunity. The various places in a value network are determined in many cases by the ability to remove transaction costs.

- There is a range of quite different activity types available to share in a perceived business opportunity. These activity types exploit different sources of declining cost economies which give rise to different ways to share in the available value added. The activity type matrix which summarises 16 sentinel activity types is presented.

Building on this foundation, the next five chapters examine topics central to the business angle perspective. These topics are:

- The demand for, and supply of, financial assets provides ways to share in a business opportunity. Contractual claims and financial markets facilitate the use of different orders of market play. Five orders of market play are described.

- The opportunity-focused business parlays its position in the market. Core competencies provide valuable scarce resources to open up new business opportunities. Five business development paths to parlay these scarce resources are described.

- Business angles are changed by the removal of friction from the value network. Reductions in transaction costs trigger changes in market structure, the capabilities undertaken within businesses and the structure of the entire value network. In accommodating the new conditions businesses transition from one activity type to another. Five market positions are described.

- The rate of market turbulence has implications for the business angle chosen, impacting on both the opportunity and appropriateness of the activity type.

- Unpredictability of the lifecycle of business opportunities also has implications for activity type in its ability to create competencies to capitalise on favourable conditions weather adverse conditions.

The final chapter discusses the application of these ideas to make best use of available resources, given the objectives of the business and market context.

ONE
Business opportunities are perceived sources of profit

The impact of unforeseen outcomes on business endeavours is a long known feature of commerce, as are the business opportunities associated with it. There are surviving documents from the Babylonian time of laws specifically formulated to recognise the cost of risk in trade. In the Middle Ages the merchant states of Northern Italy advanced the development of contract, which passed risk associated with long distance sea trade to different parties. Allied to this, and also associated with shipping was the development of sharing the high capital cost of ships through shares, typically between 24 and 64 shares. These practices were formalised through the mercantile court system in Western Europe. The rise of standardised capital and risk sharing contracts and schemes in early seventeenth century England provided clearing houses through which these contracts were traded - the most famous of these being the London Stock Exchange and Lloyd's of London. London rose to become the centre of trading companies, and maritime insurance. Not only did business risk-sharing and access to capital facilitate overseas trade, it created new business opportunities in banking, insurance and other financial services. Arguably, these developments in turn also facilitated Victorian Britain's imperialist commercial activities such as those of Cecil Rhodes in Southern Africa. The British South Africa Company gained a charter to exploit the mineral resources of what are now Zambia and Zimbabwe as a speculative commercial venture, offering shares in 1889 traded on the London Stock Exchange. Despite not paying a dividend until 1920, most of the promoters of this venture profited from the sale of their shares at the expense of later investors and the local inhabitants.

Introduction

Business opportunities are perceived sources of profit. Profit is made simultaneously by processing inputs into products that are sold for a price greater than the cost of inputs, and speculating on changes in the prices of those products and inputs.

The budget formulation process sets targets for the expected profit. These targets, usually documented in a business plan, are estimates and embody some investment in a capacity to respond to changes in market context and to seize new opportunities, and carry some degree of uncertainty on whether targets will be met. The outturn of the capacity to respond may not be fully understood, and uncertainty cannot be fully specified to account for all possible future events and actions. It is only after the event that actual profit is determined. Even then, with uncertainty eliminated, the calculation of profit provides no explanation of what created it, or information about whether that level of return is appropriate for the business given the actual circumstances that the business faced. Without knowledge of what creates profit, businesspeople using a profit target are in an endless race chasing their tail. A more useful approach to assessing a business's position is its value, which places the realisation of the perceived opportunity at the nub of the evaluation of performance.

The approach taken in this chapter is to discuss the concepts of free cash flow value (FCF value), and then elaborate on its application to understanding business opportunities. The chapter begins with an explanation of the ways in which profit is calculated. This is followed by an examination of the use made of capacities to respond to change and to ensure that business plans are met, and their implications on business opportunities as perceived sources of profit.

Source of a business's value

Scarce resources and speculation

Business opportunities are wide-ranging in their origins. Some are associated with satisfying needs of buyers, some with changing a market, some with reducing costs, while others with sharing in the flow of money. Some are also associated with the attainment of a vision offering new products to yet-to-be-developed markets. Whatever the origin, there is an expectation of a return from committing resources in pursuit of that opportunity. Placing the business opportunity at the centre of the profit calculation gives recognition to the fact that it is the operational implementation of the opportunity that is the drive of business. This hunt for business opportunities, and how to profit from them, is at the heart of the creative processes embodied in commerce.

Profit is explained as being generated from scarce resources the business has available and decisions made on the ways to act and participate in the market. In short, profit arises because the business has scarce resources and successfully engages in speculation, which can be represented as a word equation:

Profit = Return on scarce resources + Return from speculation

The expected profit from seizing an opportunity, which changes with circumstances and over time, derives from these two sources: income generating scarce resources; and gains from speculation due to changes in market prices. Scarce resources encapsulate the engagement of businesses in productive endeavours as happens in manufacturing, farming and the provision of services, for example. The speculative element recognises the possibility of gain from price changes of products and inputs. This speculative element is an integral component of business endeavours. It applies to any and all businesses.

Both elements exist simultaneously in every opportunity and contribute in different proportions. The relative sizes of the contributions cannot be known with certainty in advance and may even be difficult to establish after the event. The dependence of the profitability of primary produce producers, such as farmers and miners, on movements in produce prices is an illustration of how intertwined these sources of profit are. In saying that it is unknowable, does not mean that businesspeople are unaware of its existence or its importance and the need to address its consequences; it just means that it is difficult to ascertain, particularly in advance when this information is most useful.

The assumption that hard work is all that is needed to succeed, is naive. 'Good, honest toil' may be a virtue but there is no guarantee it will be profitable. All commerce involves some component of speculation – frequently not even recognised for what it is. The mix is changed through the way in which the business opportunity is pursued, but the impact cannot be entirely eliminated. Moreover, that impact changes over time, again in ways that are unknowable in advance.

Time and ignorance are the reasons that the degree of speculation intrinsic to an opportunity is not apparent at the outset. Knowledge of changes, and structural imperfections in the market is incomplete. This is especially the case before a business enters a market. Once a business enters the market, it must contend with other participants who seek to change that market in ways that increase their own ability to extract value added or change their exposure to risk. All businesses must contend with information deficiencies. They may adopt approaches to ameliorate information deficiencies which lower risk in planned activities. They may also use a variety of methods to gain the required information, such as using surrogate indicators or inferring the knowledge held by others from their behaviour. This transfer of knowledge from other parties by their behaviour applies to suppliers, buyers, providers of substitutes and competitors. In some cases this may involve engineering situations, such as tender processes, to force a behavioural response from the party with the knowledge, which can provide information from which to infer the knowledge they hold.

But this relationship between perceived sources of uncertainty and its management is not a simple one. As an illustration of this, a sense of greater assurance about realising the outcome of planned activities can distort the business's views about its exposure to, and therefore preparedness for, unknowable events. In this sense they are unplanned uncertainty events. In dealing with uncertainty all businesses must also contend with the possibility of imperfect decisions. A prevalent example of this is cognitive bias as a result of the sunk cost fallacy, under which recovery of past invested capital is a strong motivation and leads to 'good money being thrown after bad'. This preoccupation with recovering past invested capital results in inappropriate decisions, in the face of evidence that it is better to recognise losses to date, and move on by evaluating alternative paths to get best value for the available scarce resources.

Specification of profit

It is well recognised that the measurement of profit is simply income less costs, or to be more precise, income less the cost of goods sold and cost of resources used in production processes - again represented as a word equation:

Profit = Income – Cost of goods sold – Cost of resources used in production processes

In the setting of exploiting perceived business opportunities, profit is the residual cash income after meeting all cash commitments. This definition of profit is the 'free cash flow'. Free cash flow is not the same as accounting profit, which is determined using prescribed accounting rules and conventions. Free cash flow is calculated from cash flows. Free cash flow is estimated from financial accounts prepared under Generally Accepted Accounting Principles (also referred to as GAAP), but accounting profit takes other matters into account. Two differences between the two methods of calculation are that free cash flow: includes the working capital required by the business; and incorporates the expenditure to maintain the income earning resources of the business as a going concern. Both of these are components of the cost of resources used in production processes.

The evaluation of the profit from a perceived opportunity in renting out real estate is used to illustrate this concept. The calculation of the prospective profit would estimate the cash income from rents, taking into account vacant periods, and any gain from the sale of the property at the end of the project. This forecast income must cover the cash outlay to acquire the property, the cost of production processes to let, manage and maintain the property, working capital requirements, and the costs incurred in utilities, fees, taxes, staff, materials and insurance.

FCF value and scarce resources

The FCF value of the business is the net present value of expected profit over the lifetime of the venture. The term 'present value' refers to the value of a future amount today after taking into account the time value of money, which is called the discount rate. 'Net' refers to the fact that the FCF value is the sum of the present value of expected profits for all time periods over a venture's lifetime. So if the discount rate (which is frequently estimated as the prevailing interest rate available to the business) is 10 percent per annum, $100 invested today will be worth $110 in one year's time and $121 in two years' time. By reversing this logic, if a business venture with a two year lifespan is forecast to generate a return of $110 at the end of year one and $121 at the end of year two then its net present value is $200.

FCF value increases as profit increases (for a constant discount rate). The scarce resources generating the increased profit will also increase in value by the same amount, as will the market value of the business. This is the case in an efficient market where there are many willing sellers and buyers who have access to appropriate information to make a rational decision and low transaction costs are involved. Where this is not the case there is a divergence between different valuations of the business and this topic is discussed in the next chapter.

Scarce resources possess this unusual property that their value changes in line with changes in profit. This is quite unlike other assets whose price is purely a function of demand and supply considerations, since scarce resources are not a cost to the business but instead embody the value of the business. They are the source of its profit, where the return from scarce resources is taken in the form of profit. The ability of scarce resources to generate a return is how their value is determined in the market. Where a market exists, scarce resources are subject to demand and supply factors. In some cases scarce resources are traded, and their value is the share of value added that they are able to capture and transfer to the new owner as profit. Where no market exists for the scarce resource it can be monetised by the sale of the business as a going concern.

FCF value of scarce resources possessed by a business is the measure of the degree of competitive advantage that a business has attained. Businesses with highly valuable scarce resources have high competitive advantage.

Interim profit and FCF value

Some ventures are established with a specified term that spans several years. In the simplest case this involves significant investment in inputs at the start of the venture, low maintenance costs over the life of the venture, then income at the end of the term when the venture is liquidated. With judicious management decisions and favourable market conditions the venture's profit is calculated at the end of the period (taking account of the time value of money in this calculation). In this example, with a single pay-out at the end of the period each of the previous years has a loss. But reporting losses each year until the final year gives no recognition of whether the opportunity perceived at the beginning of the venture is progressively being realised. One way to achieve this is to recalculate the FCF value at the end of each year. The change in FCF value over the year, less the costs incurred, is the profit for the year.

While this method of calculating profit is firmly focused on realising the business opportunity, it nonetheless is at odds with the calculation of profit using GAAP. The reason for this is that the point of view taken in the calculation of accounting profit is to document the source and application of funds, which is an historic view of transactions. The difference between these two approaches is illustrated by the treatment of investment in resources. In the accounting treatment, return on the purchase price of assets is deemed a meaningful measure, whereas, from the opportunity point-of-view it is the contribution of those resources to FCF value that is important.

To further illustrate this concept, utility infrastructure businesses are established with the intention that once the resources are in place they will have a very long lifespan. Provided the resource is well maintained and there is no change in revenue or operating costs from one period to the next, the FCF value will remain unchanged from one period to another, at least in the short-term. Profit would be zero, and cash covering all cash commitments including maintaining resources would be zero. A positive profit would indicate that expected conditions in the future have improved the profitability of the businesses, and the converse would apply. While the change may be anticipated to occur, the impact on profit is recognised when this knowledge becomes known. Where profit is zero, accounting profit is likely to be positive because depreciation, which is based on historic costs, will be lower than the investment needed to maintain the future income earning ability of the infrastructure. Businesses that earn zero profit return an amount equal to the discount rate to owners. Most businesses stumble along with an FCF value that is next to nothing. For these businesses, and making the assumption that they are going concerns, for practical purposes profit is the net income of the period (with book value depreciation used as an estimate of the cost of maintaining the income earning capability of resources). To avoid this confusion and to exploit a market opening requires profit to be correctly calculated. This is best achieved by using free cash flow assumptions.

Capacity to respond to events, and endure the consequences of time and ignorance

In the example of the real estate rental business given above, it is easy to estimate the incomes and costs involved. Some elements of uncertainty - those that impact on estimates - can be identified and steps taken to manage them. As an aside, uncertainties are generally referred to in everyday speech as risks, although risk is a particular type of uncertainty. (The concept of uncertainty is discussed in more detail later.) However, uncertainty will remain around estimates, in part because future prices are unknown, in part because of miscalculations of the market opportunity; and in part because the knowhow, systems, processes and other arrangements put in place turn out to operate differently from what was planned. (This could be due to unforeseeable failures and accident.) The cost of uncertainty can also stem from inappropriate decisions, the business being taken advantage of by a supplier (frequently because performance is difficult to assess), and the difficulty of distinguishing good products from bad ones at the time of purchase resulting in a lower price of good products. The uncertainty premium also covers lucky breaks from identifying opportunities from which the business may benefit. The cost necessary to ensure that the business plan is realised is the uncertainty premium.

Businesses can also choose to invest (or divest) resources to increase (or reduce) the capacity to provide the flexibility to deal with future adverse market conditions, or to be in a position to seize new opportunities that emerge. Decisions to not commit resources, or the timing and size of any commitment, are decisions to choose options. An option is the cost of holding open choices that will enable the business to respond to circumstances, and in that way enhance future income earning ability from scarce resources, without the obligation of having to undertake a specific course of action. Tradable option contracts and real options are the two general types of options. Both types involve a cost and this application of income is the option premium.

A tradeable option contract involves the purchaser of the option paying a fee (the option premium for the purchaser) for the right to buy (called a call option) or sell (this is a put option) a real or financial asset at a specified price. This approach offers certainty of a future price and is widely used by businesses to fix foreign currency prices, for example. These contracts are time-bound and can be exercised at any time before or on the specified date, otherwise the option expires. The purchaser of the option is not obliged to exercise it. Where the conditions of the contract allow, the purchaser can sell the option before it expires to a third party. The option premium for the seller who writes a tradable option contract is the income received, and for the buyer the option premium is the current price of the unexpired tradable option contract.

Options are also used to give flexibility over non-financial transactions. A real option is the right but not the obligation to undertake some real business activity, such as constructing or selling a building. The option of constructing the building is a real call option, and selling the building is a real put option. Unlike tradable option contracts, real options, in general, cannot be traded as financial securities and may not be precisely time-bound. Here the option premium is the cost of holding the option open. Keeping with the real estate example, having bought land to create an option to build in the future, the business incurs costs by continuing to own the land because of the time value of money and other costs incurred while it is vacant. This cost declines over time as the remaining time before sale diminishes. The option ceases to exist when the decision is executed, and the option premium therefore becomes zero.

A full specification of income and costs would recognise a premium to cover uncertainty, and a premium to gain flexibility to deal with the wide range of conditions that could occur in the market, in order to enhance the income earning ability of the business. Summarising this, business planning and budgeting requires decisions in four areas that are related in the following way:

Forecast income = Forecast cost + Option premium + Premium for uncertainty

Portfolio of salient strategic options and risk mitigants

The return on scarce resources and speculation is the outturn from the actual use of resources to capture a share of the available value added for the business. The aim of the business plan is to set out: how scarce resources are to be created, enhanced and applied operationally; the competitive actions to be taken; and the timing and nature of strategic decisions to be made.

In the planning stage, options remain open, and the cost of holding them open is the option premium. As the business plan is executed, the portfolio of options changes and the option premium changes. The same applies to risk mitigation arrangements put in place.

The option and uncertainty premiums give recognition to the portfolio of salient strategic options, risk mitigation arrangements and constraints that the business faces in participating in markets. Even where these are not explicitly managed, businesses are continually changing the composition of this portfolio of options and arrangements. This occurs in parallel with changes in the mix of constraints that are faced. Some of these options, mitigants and constraints remain relevant and roll over from one period to the next. Some new options and constraints will be acquired or incurred. Some options will be exercised or allowed to expire, mitigants will be invested in and changed, and constraints will change or be removed. This process of managing a portfolio of options, mitigants and constraints is one of the key roles of management. While the maintenance of options and mitigants comes at a cost, the payback is from the increase in FCF value from improved future returns and certainty of achieving plans and budgets.

Business involves continuously exercising numerous strategic options. While each individual option has its own option premium, in this discussion the term option premium is used to mean the aggregate premium of all the options available to a particular business. The same logic applies to uncertainty, and the uncertainty premium is the aggregate of all risk mitigation arrangements the business has put in place at a particular point in time.

For positive FCF value, forecast cash inflow (e.g. the sales, dividends, rents received) must cover all forecast cash outflow commitments (including tax) from planned decisions on the timing and use of inputs available to the business (the costs) to earn that income. There will be uncertainties around these incomes and costs and the timings of when they are received or incurred. The forecast income must take this into account, by means of a premium for uncertainty. These uncertainties are a normal part of being in business and many are outside of its control. The forecast cost includes the cost of resources allocated to maintaining the on-going income earning ability of the business. This cost is depreciation. It stands distinct from resources applied to increasing (or reducing) the capacity to earn and realise the expected profit by having the flexibility to respond to future market conditions, which is investment (or disinvestment). This application of income is the option premium.

Business plans and budgets do not usually separately identify the income and costs associated with option and uncertainty premiums. Instead the impact of uncertainty and the capacity to enhance profits are frequently incorporated by developing different scenarios. These scenarios model perceived different risks and market circumstances.

A simple way to account for the components of uncertainty on profitability is by modelling the likelihood of a business achieving different levels of profitability;

for example, if the forecast base case profit for a venture is $100, 25 percent less if the business slightly undershoots its target, and 100 per cent less in a worst case scenario. If the expected likelihood of each alternative occurring is 60 percent, 30 percent and 10 percent, respectively, then the expected level of profit is $82.50 (being $100 x 60% + $100 x (100% – 25%) x 30% = $82.50). Adjusting the base case profit ($100) for an approximation of uncertainty results in the expected profit ($82.50). This $17.50 difference between base case and expected profit is an estimate of the premium for uncertainty. This calculation relies on finding estimates of the alternative scenarios and the likelihood of their occurrence. Alternatively the premium for risk is expressed as a percentage, in this example, of 17.5 percent. An analogous method is used to estimate the option premium provided by the portfolio of strategic options put in place. How realistic these estimates are will only be known after the event.

This method of calculating the expected profit from a venture is used to estimate the expected FCF value by applying the above logic to each of the future year's profit to be included in the valuation, and discounting the future profits by the time value of money. To simplify the valuation process, frequently only the base case is estimated for each of the multiple years, and the uncertainty premium is incorporated into the discount rate that is applied to the business – giving a risk adjusted discount rate.

Sometimes the planned initiatives to provide flexibility and risk mitigating mechanisms are described in the business plan. Frequently these are not. Businesses facing cash flow pressures or pressures to pay high dividends commonly address this by reducing expenditure on maintenance of resources. This reduces their income earning capacity and is a negative option premium.

After the time period and events covered in the business plan have occurred, the actual income and cost are known for the decisions that were made. At that point it is usually impossible to separately distinguish the components of income and cost attributed to planned activity, flexibility, risk mitigation or serendipity. There are occasions when the impact of the occurrence of specific market conditions can be identified. It is rare that the impacts of risk and serendipity are scrutinised.

Challenges embodied in time and ignorance

As portrayed here, time and ignorance challenge the creation of high value scarce resources. Time and ignorance force businesspeople to address and institute mechanisms to ensure business plans and budgets are realised. The flipside of this is that these same forces also provide business opportunities that can be monetised through speculation. From yet another perspective, time and ignorance challenge businesses to find ways to ensure continuity over time by parlaying existing resources into new opportunities. Investing in capacity to do this, in turn, provides the business with another way to monetise opportunities, this time through speculative opportunities that derive from time and ignorance. The mechanisms to address these challenges and opportunities for creating FCF value are interwoven.

This interweaving is illustrated by the place of research and development (R&D) in businesses. R&D on production processes is used to improve reliability of finished products and reduce cost of rework, and in this way improve the certainty of achieving production and service cost targets – helping to create a scarce resource. R&D that results in innovative use of low cost feedstock, for example as an input into production capabilities, enables the business to play the market to get the most economical price for this input – providing an opportunity to speculate on inputs in order to achieve input cost targets with more certainty. R&D that is used to innovate higher productivity production processes (which includes organisational structures) also creates capacity to respond to competitive challenges – extending the on-going viability of the scarce resource. Such innovation could also provide capacity to respond to serendipity and parlay the businesses position in the market – an option to speculate. Time and ignorance create multiple challenges for businesses, impacting on the magnitude of the uncertainty and option premiums, as well as creating new opportunities to make use of the available scarce resources and for speculation.

Scarce resources can potentially be created for all business opportunities. A normal part of commerce is to plan to take a position on future impacts of time and ignorance in the markets in which the business operates. Competencies are required to do this, but these may not develop into scarce resources. To develop scarce resources, businesses have to invest in mechanisms to improve the certainty of meeting plans and budgets by investing in capacity to enable business continuity. Businesses use production processes, together with organisational structure, made up of activity type, capabilities, and contractual obligations to achieve this.

The capacity to respond and risk mitigation mechanisms have different roles to perform. Because both require the commitment of resources, decisions made in respect of either one can also impact on the other. For example, to minimise capital requirements a business may choose to outsource some capacity and capabilities. With an appropriate contract, this may also provide the business with the ability to scale up capacity, if required. On the other hand, outsourcing this capability means that the business is unable to build scarce resources in that area. Were that capability to emerge as a scarce resource, the outsourced supplier may capture a disproportionate share of the value added.

Although the option and uncertainty premiums are different in their objectives, decisions made to manage each can impact on the other. Which matters a business sees as falling within the scope of its option and uncertainty premiums will depend on the business angle it has adopted. While volatility in prices may be a problem for one business, challenging the creation of scarce resources, for another business it may be a business opportunity in which scarce resources are created. One business's capability in speculation is another business's capability in a scarce resource.

Summary

A business opportunity embodies the expectation of earning a return on the resources committed. Part of the opportunity comes from processing inputs into products that can be sold for a price greater that the cost, and part from speculation of changes in prices of products and inputs. The simplified rendering of this is that for the set of capabilities possessed by the business:

Profit = Return on scarce resources + Return on speculation

The value of scarce resources changes in line with changes in profit, as well as demand and supply factors. This is unlike other assets whose price is a function of demand and supply considerations.

Uncertainty is a cost faced by all businesses and impacts on profitability. Like many other aspects of commerce, the size of this cost is unknown in advance, even though its key drivers may be known. The option premium reflects the cost of holding open choices that will enable the business to respond to circumstances and enhance the future income earning ability of scarce resources. The uncertainty premium reflects the contingency necessary to ensure that the business plan is realised. In business planning and budgeting, a full specification of the situation a business faces is:

Forecast income = Forecast costs + Option premium + Premium for uncertainty

Here profit is the residual income over the investment horizon after meeting all cash outflow commitments (the costs).

To varying degrees businesses strive to create high value scarce resources. Time and ignorance challenge this because mechanisms are required to ensure that business plans and budgets are realised. The forces of time and ignorance also provide business opportunities that can be monetised through speculation. In addition, time and ignorance impose challenges to ensure continuity over time by parlaying existing resources into new opportunities. Investing in capacity to respond, in turn, provides through speculation another way to monetise opportunities that derive from time and ignorance. The mechanisms to address challenges and opportunities stemming from time and ignorance are interwoven.

Selected literature review

Early origin of idea

John Maynard Keynes in *The General Theory of Employment, Interest and Money* (published first in 1936 by Macmillan and available in more recent reprints) writes that ignorance of what the future holds is the outstanding fact, and in making an investment businesspeople "play a mixed game of skill and chance, the average results of which to the participants are not known by those who take a hand". Keynes' view is that investment involves judgements by businesspeople, and judgements about an opportunity have to be confronted anew with each opportunity. Despite the limitations in calculating future outturn from an investment, the act of trying to pick a winner by speculating is an integral feature of commerce. This led Keynes to describe a situation in which businesspeople continually seek new ways through which to profit from perceived market opportunities. This hunt is both on-going and dynamic as businesspeople are forced also to anticipate the behaviour of others. Keynes describes the notion of an uncertain future and a vigorous hunt by businesspeople to discover some angle, or gap in the market. The expected profit comes from picking and making the investment in resources and other assets for an acceptable expected return, taking into account uncertainty. In making the investment, part of the return is the yield from enterprise, and part from the speculative behaviour of other investors changing the price of assets.

Key influences on the work

The logic that profit is due to scarce resources is set out by Lippman and Rumelt in their 2003 papers 'The Payments Perspective: Micro-Foundations of Resource Analysis' and 'The Bargaining Perspective on resource advantage', both published in the *Strategic Management Journal*.

That risk is a cost to business is put forward in 'The Risk Sharing Strawman' by Makholm in the July 1988 edition of *Public Utilities*. There is much writing on speculation, and an accessible exploration is provided by Shiller in *The New Financial Order: Risk in the 21st Century* published in 2004 by Princeton University Press. Most textbooks on corporate finance explain the calculation of value of a business on the basis of net cash flow. One text is Damodaran's 1996 book *Investment Valuation: Tools and techniques for determining the value of any asset* published by John Wiley & Sons. Options are also discussed in corporate finance textbooks, see for example Hull *Options, Futures, and other Derivatives* published by Prentice-Hall International in 2000.

TWO
Businesses share in the available value added

The company Bolton and Watt was formed in 1775 to exploit the patent awarded to James Watt for his significant improvements to the steam engine. By all measures this new engine was much more efficient than alternatives available at the time. Patent protection was actively enforced by the company to reduce competition. Having successfully disrupted the market for steam engines, and establishing a position in the market with strong bargaining power, Bolton and Watt set out to capture value added from businesses that depended on steam power. They achieved this by sharing in the resulting savings in the cost of coal to the business as a consequence of the use of their steam engine. The price of an installed and maintained steam engine was a share of the saving in the cost of coal achieved by their engine compared with the alternative less efficient steam engines they were replacing.

Introduction

To pursue a perceived business opportunity businesspeople have to work through four sets of interrelated considerations: the size and scope of investment, and level of risk and return to accept; which markets to participate in; where to position in the value network to extract value; and what capabilities to use to do this. But this is not the end of the story. The decisions made by participants change the flow of money, and the weight of the flow of money changes the configuration of markets, and as a consequence, the business opportunities available. The profitable solution to the four sets of interrelated considerations is always in flux because of changes by the market participants, the influence of external factors, and variations in the flow of capital to participants. These fluctuations at times can be substantial. In the absence of impediments, this state of flux itself provides business opportunities. Knowledge that markets can change, and be influenced by change, provides further business opportunities. Businesspeople have a broad canvas for the identification of opportunities and the design of business angles.

How businesses participate in markets in order to capture value added is set out in this chapter. It does this by describing the business in the context of the various markets in which it operates. This chapter starts with an explanation of the markets in which businesses participate and how value added is allocated across the various stages in a value network. This is followed by a discussion of how value added is allocated between competitive alternatives at a stage in the value network.

Participating in markets

The allocation of value added

Businesses capture a share of the value added created by a value network. This share is the business's profit. An explanation of how value added is shared between the different participants in the value network is as follows; buyers consider the perceived benefit of a product less its price - this is the value-for-money provided by the product. This assessment is done for each of the alternatives available to, and affordable by, the buyer; who then chooses the product offering the greatest value-for-money. This is the subjective assessment of the difference between the bundles of benefits received from the purchase offset by the price. The range of products considered by a buyer is limited by the budget available to spend. A wide range of perceived benefits are considered by buyers, including aspirational benefits such as its allure within the context and culture in which the product is offered for sale. One of the tasks of a business is to influence buyers' perception of wants, value-for-money and availability, and thereby to increase the sales of its products.

Managing the delivery of perceived benefit to buyers in a manner that increases the price received is one part of the profit equation. The other part of the equation is to increase surplus on the inputs purchased. For the producer this is the value-for-money from acquiring inputs. Profit arises where the price realised from sales is more than the price paid for all inputs used (the costs). Businesses, as buyers of inputs, apply the same processes as other buyers in making decisions on the purchase of inputs, namely to increase perceived benefit, which is the difference between the benefit and the cost. The perceived benefit to the business is the contribution of the input to the objectives of the business, and the price and conditions of sale accepted for the inputs. This is another of the tasks of a business - the management of capabilities for the creation of perceived benefit from acquired inputs.

A value network consists of clusters of suppliers and providers that culminate in the delivery of a product to the final buyer. High level allocation of value added on a single unit of a product in a simple value network is presented in Figure 1 for a provider, with suppliers selling to buyers. Buyers pay a price for the product and enjoy value-for-money from its consumption. The business's surplus is the profit on a single unit of the product. In this depiction suppliers also enjoy a surplus, or unit profit. However, where the supplier is labour then there is no surplus, only the price of that input. The total of the surpluses is the unit value added created by the value network. In this depiction, 65 percent of the unit value added is taken by final consumers, 20 percent by the provider and 15 percent by the supplier. Unit profit is the share of unit value added captured by suppliers and the provider.

Figure 1 *Bar graph depicting the allocation of value added from a single unit of a product in a value network consisting of buyer, provider and supplier*

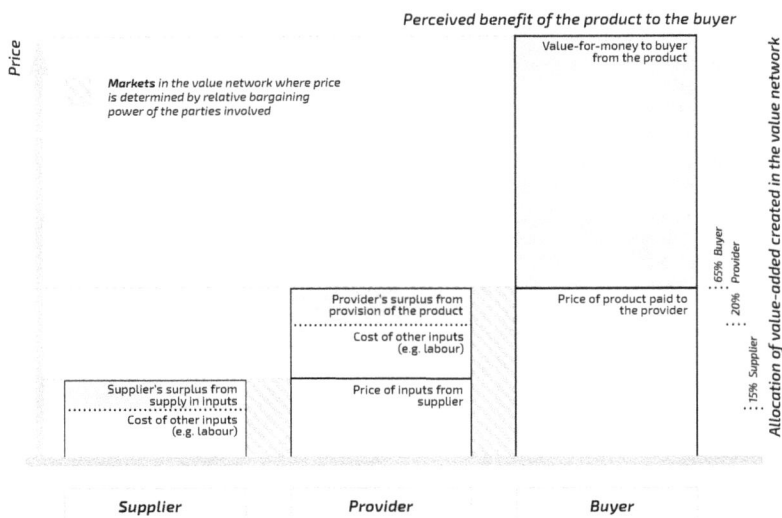

Perceived benefit of the product to the buyer

Price

Markets *in the value network where price is determined by relative bargaining power of the parties involved*

Value-for-money to buyer from the product

Provider's surplus from provision of the product
....
Cost of other inputs
(e.g. labour)

Price of product paid to the provider

Supplier's surplus from supply in inputs
....
Cost of other inputs
(e.g. labour)

Price of inputs from supplier

65% Buyer
20% Provider
15% Supplier

Allocation of value-added created in the value network

Supplier   Provider   Buyer

Business decisions are not this straight-forward. For example, to make matters more challenging, information on the final sale price, and indeed the perceived benefit, is unknown even at the time it is offered for sale, although in many instances it is treated as known, being advertised at a fixed sales price, until the sale actually takes place. Even in these cases, the knowledge of the future sales price is uncertain. In addition, future prices of inputs are difficult to ascertain. To deal with this uncertainty, the market forms expectations about prices. The reason the sale price is so difficult to estimate is that it is the price struck on exchange between the seller and buyer. The process by which this price is established can be thought of as follows. Potential buyers consider the perceived benefit to them, which could involve other consequential decision such as the on-sale of the product, and will choose that provider able to offer the greatest value-for-money. This choice involves consideration of alternatives, complements, budget constraints, bargaining power and perceptions about the future. Sellers seek to influence the size of this perceived benefit, by targeting potential buyers, structuring the payments to fit budget constraints, advertising, product design and packaging, and service delivery, positioning to change the view of alternatives and complements, and increasing their bargaining power. Exactly what price is struck between the buyers' willingness to pay and the price acceptable to the seller depends on their relative bargaining power within the market context.

Element markets of market opportunities

This process of buyers choosing suppliers and setting prices occurs in each of the markets in which a business operates. A depiction of some of the markets in which businesses operate is provided in Figure 2. Expected revenue is determined by the comparative value-for-money offered by the products available, which in turn is a function of product attributes and the alternatives available to the buyer, amongst other things. The actual choice of inputs (which include commodities and assets) is determined by the value added that the business can gain from them. The price paid is influenced by price paid by competitors. In addition, a significant component of the cost of inputs is the cost of uncertainty. Regulatory and institutional arrangements in the form of social conventions, the law and agreements are widely used as ways to assign some risks to parts of a sale and purchase agreement.

A crucial market in which businesses operate is that of contractual commitments, which can take the form of supply arrangements, risk sharing, options, lending and debt contracts. Contractual commitments arise from express terms and conditions between the parties to an agreement, and are the foundation on which financial assets are built. Financial assets are created from assets and liabilities transacted in each of the element markets in which a business operates. Some elements of product risk can be contracted to rest with the buyer, but nonetheless, there are elements of risk that are a cost to the business through regulatory and institutional arrangements, and product design. Elements of this risk can be passed onto other parties, for example, through insurance.

Another source of income is that which results from the increase in price of assets. Businesses can trade and create assets as by-products in the course of their business activities. A notable example, owing to the price they can sell for, are assets such as brand and intellectual property. Liabilities can also be created, for instance, contaminated land, water and air, as well as product liability claims. These created assets can be worth more to other parties than to the business that created them. The sale of rights to use these assets is a significant source of income for some businesses (usually categorised in financial accounts prepared under GAAP as extraordinary non-recurring income).

Figure 2 places the element markets that contribute to a business's value in the context of market prices. The diagram shows that a business operates in at least five markets. These markets are for buyers of its products, sellers of inputs including labour, scarce resources, other assets and liabilities controlled or owned by the business, and shares from investors in the business as a going concern. In the search for an angle on a business opportunity businesspeople seek to exploit changes in market context faced by any of these element markets. Investment of resources is the consequence of there being businesspeople who perceive an opportunity and are prepared to commit resources to pursue it. The depiction in Figure 2 identifies a number of examples of changes in market context that impact business value. Each of these can contribute to improving the business's FCF value. These contributors are:

- **Contributor 1** Providing products whose value-for-money is greater than alternatives. Improving value-for-money is required to grow revenue.
- **Contributor 2** Selecting a set of inputs to support a high productivity production process through economical purchase of those inputs.
- **Contributor 3** Making valuable scarce resources from a high productivity production process delivering planned outputs.
- **Contributor 4** Providing risk mitigants to ensure that business plans are met, and strategic options, to provide the reliance for on-going profitability.
- **Contributor 5** Enhancing business value by financial management, including maintaining alignment between FCF value and the market price of the business.

A corollary of this is that businesses shed assets that do not contribute to the creation of scarce resources. Legal, regulatory and institutional arrangements impact the value of a business through this contributor.

Businesses routinely and actively improve and innovate in these five areas. A business opportunity arises when one, or any combination of, these contributors can be changed in a way that improves the value of the business. Under this formulation, value is the payment received by the business for the choice and implementation of a business angle. These decisions create valuable scarce resources, and placing the business in a market also emphasises that profit is the payment received for the business's scarce resources.

Businesses increase FCF value through innovations and market interventions, which increase the share of revenue captured by the business and ultimately by the business's owners. This occurs where the innovation or intervention increases the scarcity value of resources that it owns or controls. From the point of view of business owners, there are three ways to improve the value of a business: create valuable scarce resources; use contractual commitments with third parties; and create equity attractive to investors.

Figure 2 *Depiction of some of the markets in which a business operates and the contributors to its value*

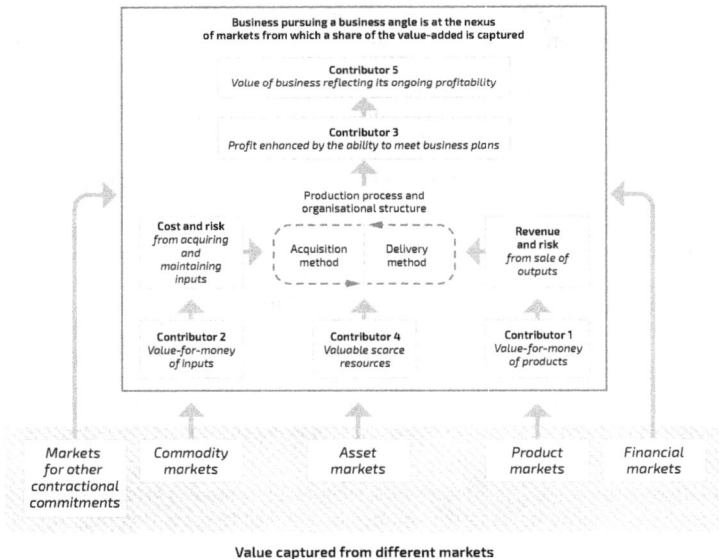

Value captured from different markets

Placing the business angle at the centre of a number of element markets shows that the definition of the market is determined by the contribution each makes to FCF value. For example, at one level businesses involved in trade resell inputs from suppliers in one market to buyers in another market. At another level, resellers operate in a different market to suppliers by creating a buyer experience - curating a range a products, service experience, and terms and conditions of sale, quite different from those provided by suppliers. In this way the resellers' product market is quite different from that faced by their suppliers. The same logic applies to the definition of asset markets, except in this case where these are used in the systems and processes to acquire inputs for transformation and delivery as products to buyers. Clearly one business's products are other businesses' commodities and assets. The classification of items into different markets according to their contribution to a business's FCF value applies to all items.

Value of a business

The fact that different markets converge in the business is exploited by different participants as a source of business opportunities. Each of the five contributors can be used to improve the FCF value of a business. Not all businesses choose to actively participate in developing the contribution of each of these markets. As an illustration, the asset market value is the value of the assets, such as land, buildings, plant and equipment, and other property rights such as patents. Some of these assets may have a market price, while others may be difficult to price or have no, or negative, price to others. Product markets can also provide assets in the form of assignable contracts. For profitable businesses, both these values should be less than the FCF value of the business. One objective is to maximise FCF value by maximising the value from assets (whether owned or partly owned) that are synergistic or involved in co-specialisation. Any assets that do not meet this test are sold, as they contribute northing to the value of the business plan.

Figure 3 is a bar graph that shows market value of a business equal to its FCF value due to its scarce resources, of which most are unpriced assets. By 'priced' is meant that the asset can be bought and sold in the market. Most assets created by profitable businesses are scarce resources, and are unpriced in the form of its core competencies.

Figure 3 *Bar graph of three valuations of a business as a going concern in an efficient market*

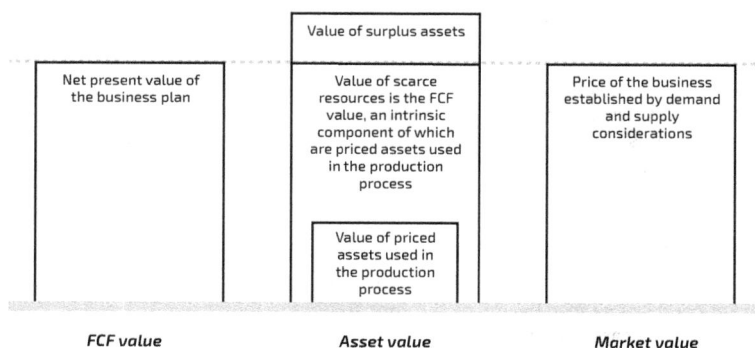

Net present value of the business plan	Value of surplus assets	Price of the business
	Value of scarce resources is the FCF value, an intrinsic component of which are priced assets used in the production process	established by demand and supply considerations
	Value of priced assets used in the production process	
FCF value	**Asset value**	**Market value**

The market value of the business, the FCF value of its scarce resources, and the price of the business's assets can be different. The implications of different combinations of FCF, priced assets and market values are:

- If the FCF value is greater than the market value, which is greater than the priced assets, then the business has unpriced scarce resources; but the business has a more optimistic assessment of the impact of uncertainty and its strategic options than is held by the market. This presents the owners of the business with a challenge to realise the value of these scarce resources, should they wish to sell them, which might be best achieved through a trade sale or management buyout.

- If the FCF value is greater than the priced assets, which is greater than the market value, then the business has a more optimistic assessment of the impact of uncertainty and its strategic options than is held by the market; and it is unclear whether the business has unpriced scarce resources. This situation can occur where the scarce resource is idiosyncratic to the owners; a situation many small businesses find themselves in where there is no effective market for the sale of the business.

- If the market value is greater than the FCF value, which is greater than the priced assets, then the business has unpriced scarce resources; but the market has a more optimistic assessment of the impact of uncertainty and its strategic options than is held by management. This could occur where there is a potential buyer able to realise value that is not available to the business under its current ownership.

- If the market value is greater than the priced assets, which is greater than the FCF value, then the market has a more optimistic assessment of the impact of uncertainty and its strategic options than is held by management, and the market believes that resources are poorly utilised. This situation would call for a review of the business angle being pursued by the business, with the possible sale of the business's assets that are worth more to others than the business as a going concern.

- If the value of the priced assets is greater than both FCF and market values, then the business is a candidate for takeover and asset stripping. Restructured, with surplus assets sold, could uncover a business angle with positive FCF value. The conclusion nonetheless remains, the business is worth more broken up and restructured than retained in its current form.

As an aside, FCF value, priced assets, and market values are likely to be very different from the book value of the initial investment and the revaluation provisions under GAAP. The possibility of different valuations provides fertile opportunities for speculation in asset and financial markets. It is in this way that financial markets are one of the element markets in which all businesses operate. There are also business opportunities associated with creating priced assets from cash flow commitments, access to resources and changing the terms and conditions of the ownership or control of assets.

Scarce resources and value capture

Scarce resources are valuable and their price increases with improvements in market conditions faced by any of the contributors to increasing FCF value. An asset is not a scarce resource, where increase in demand can be met by purchasing more of it at the same, or possibly better, prices through pecuniary economies. Such assets are inputs, for example, plant and machinery. They are not scarce resources, but can form part of systems and processes of a capability, which is a core competency. Core competencies are scarce resources.

Grounding the business in a number of markets provides insight into how the available value added, in a value network, is allocated between the stages in the value network. This allocation is up to the value added at that stage in the value network. Having said this, it can also be zero. Resource scarcity increases the share of value added captured by the business. A coarse allocation of value added is determined by the incursion of markets into the value network to create stages in the value network. It does this by providing the reference point for assessing value-for-money. In this way, the market provides a first cut allocation of value added between stages in the value network. Markets also provide high level insight into the available sources of value added in the market.

From this starting point the next consideration is the allocation of value added between the participants in the value network. There is no easy way to measure value-for-money to buyers, although it existence (modified by the cost of friction) is revealed through sales and market share. The allocation of value added to a party is determined by the comparative value-for-money of the alternatives available to the 'buyer" (in each of the markets), the capacity constraints in meeting demand, and strength of the preference for buyers and suppliers to work together.

In practice there is no simple calculation of the net impact of this set of factors on bargaining power of the parties. Where there are several suppliers competing for the available buyers, then buyers can take a large share of the value added in the form of a large value-for-money. The same process occurs in the purchase of inputs. Indeed, the same process of allocation of value added between participants occurs in each market. In highly unfavourable markets where the business has no ability, at least in the short-term, to reposition its products, it must focus its efforts on increasing profitability by being more efficient and using cheaper inputs, and by making use of appropriate contractual commitments. This might involve innovating and investing in capabilities that utilise less labour. The failure to achieve a surplus in any of these areas means that there is no opportunity cost to the business from its use of scarce resources and other inputs.

While the product market is used in this illustration, this set of considerations applies in each value network of which the business is a member. In each market the available value added is allocated to each of the parties. In a simple case there may be a thin, or no, market for the ownership of the business or for its assets, and financial markets may simply share in the available value added by providing secured debt finance to the business. In some cases, these other markets may add to the value captured by the business, for example, where the willingness to pay for the purchase of the business or its assets is greater than the FCF value from continued ownership.

The allocation of value added between competitors

Market size

To estimate a business's expected revenue requires knowledge of market demand, and in particular the relationship between price and sales quantity – a relationship shown in a demand curve in which price determines the level of sales. Analysis of demand curves and cost structures is essential for the design of a business angle that has some prospect of sharing in the value added at a particular stage in a value network. This knowledge is required to establish: whether a business has or has any prospect of developing core competencies, and the likely market share and competitor responses. This knowledge is also required to establish the appropriate price for the benefit associated with the product.

Establishing an appropriate price is a particular problem faced by start-ups taking new products to market as it requires a clear understanding of the comparative benefit of the product.

It is easily observed that products have different benefits and sell at different prices. It is also easily observed that some similar products compete directly with one another and that some position themselves for particular group of buyers – a market segment. Businesses do this as a way to improve their access to a share of the available value added. Also germane to the calculation of market size is the definition of the market. A narrow definition, for example, increases market share.

In a market consisting of a single product with the same benefit attributes sold into separate market segments, the aggregate market demand is obtained by adding horizontally the quantity demanded by each buyer of the product at different prices. This gives the total size of the market at different prices. The left hand graph in Figure 4 shows demand curves for three distinct market segments (segments A, B and C) where each segment is different in size and price elasticity of demand (which is taken to be constant). Price elasticity of demand is a measure of the proportionate change in quantity demanded as a result of a proportionate small change in price. Adding these three demand curves horizontally gives the aggregate market demand curve in the right hand graph. The aggregate market demand curve gives the size of the market.

The converse also applies. Where a business is able to segment the market, it changes the apparent price elasticity of demand and market size of the segments, for the segment and the remainder of the market.

Figure 4 *Demand curves for three separate market segments in which a product is sold, and the aggregate market demand curve*

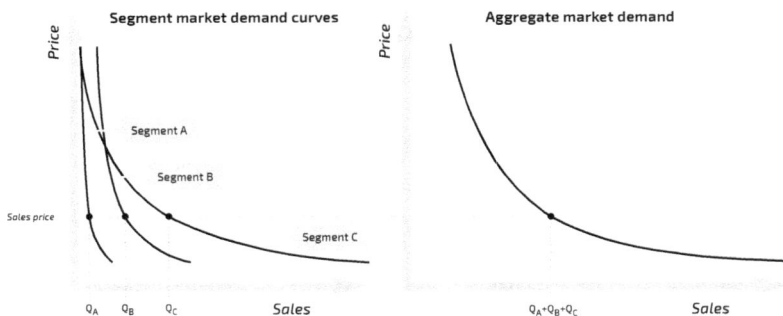

Groups of buyers (market segments) are created through the following factors:

- Designing products with attributes desirable by a target group of buyers, and which differentiate the product from competing products.
- Disposable income and budget constraints on the part of buyers.
- Barriers due to imperfect information, distance, transaction cost, fixed cost and cost of market entry.
- Legal and other institutional restrictions, such as consumer protection and intellectual property regimes. These restrictions differ between jurisdictions.

- Availability of substitutes and links with complements.
- Advertising and brand loyalty, which in turn can create product meaning.
- Restrictions on arbitrage, such as the ability to keep groups of buyers separate (e.g. physical identification of products, contract and technology locks and integration in supporting systems).
- Tastes that change over time, and familiarity and experience from using the product.
- Availability in time and place.

The ability to segment, and to combine segments, presents opportunities to businesses to improve their capture of a share of value added. For example, segmenting a market provides a way to reduce the number of competitors. To shape the market to best advantage a range of ways to segment a market are used; but creating and maintaining a segment comes at a cost.

To give context to this discussion on market share, various competitive scenarios are explored in the following discussion. One market positioning strategy used by businesses is to set out to develop a market segment in which it is the dominant provider. A determined new entrant into the market with this dominant player (offering a similar product at a similar price) might seek to goad the dominant player to respond in such a way so as to legitimise the new entrant as a competitor in the eyes of buyers. The end result the new entrant seeks to achieve is to gain market share from the dominant player.

The dominant player's response may instead be to corral the new entrant. It can do this by introducing a competing product to that of the new entrant, causing the new entrant to have to compete with this new product. This in effect creates a new segment containing the new market products. Through this strategy, the incumbent aims to use the new entrant to help open up and develop a new market segment, and to split the new market with the new entrant while keeping the new entrant away from the home segment.

Although business opportunities are perceived sources of profit, profit realisation requires consideration of how the business is to share in the available value added with other participants in the market, and there are a number of ways this is achieved. Possibilities available to a new entrant are to create a new segment, or compete for market share within an existing segment, or disrupt the market entirely. Creating a new segment is a competitive strategy available where the value-for-money offered by the new entrant is similar to that of the incumbent, and head-on competition is possible. Here, an entry strategy is to offer compatibility with the dominant player's offering and cherry-pick high value customers. Whereas, for a market-disrupting product offered by the new entrant, to which the incumbent is unlikely to be able to respond, the appropriate strategy is to make the disrupting product incompatible with the legacy product, leaving it isolated. These examples show that market segmentation is important competitive strategy available to businesses.

Market share

Businesses make a place in the market to share in the available value added. Market share is distributed between participants on the basis of the strength of market segmentation factors, and supply considerations.

The supply curve shows the average cost and market share of each supplier in a market. In a competitive market, with many suppliers of the same product, the supply curve is constructed by ordering the producers from lowest to highest average cost and for each price from highest to lowest sales. A depiction of a supply curve for a competitive market, with three suppliers with capacity constraints (referred to as A, B and C), is shown in Figure 5. The market share of each business is set by the business's available capacity and average cost. The market price is set by the highest cost producer able to survive and remain in the market (this is supplier C). The share of the value added gained by a business is the difference between the price and average cost.

High price elasticity of demand is associated with weak product differentiation and more competition. In a competitive market the price elasticity of demand faced by a business is high. This is demonstrated by the impact of a reduction in price by supplier A in Figure 5. Suppler A is the most efficient user of resources to generate sales and were it to increase capacity and maintain or reduce its average cost, and reduce its price, it could gain market share. Supplier A would experience a proportionately high improvement in sales (of Q) for a small proportionate price decrease – in other words it will find the market highly price elastic. In Figure 5, supplier A's increase in sales is at the detriment of the most inefficient supplier (C).

The aggregate price elasticity of demand cannot be imputed from the experiences of a single business. To estimate the price elasticity of demand for the entire market requires estimates of the sales, price and benefit attributes of each competitor.

As a broad statement, producers increase profit by increasing production efficiency, and when faced with declining costs from increased capacity, this is accompanied by an increase in market share.

Figure 5 *Demand and supply curves and the impact on market share of a reduction in price by one competitor in a competitive market*

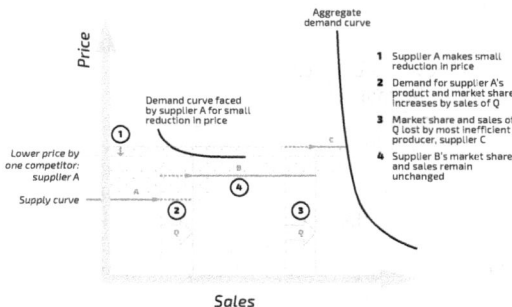

Product differentiation

The more usual situation encountered is to find similar products with differences in some attributes selling at different prices. Sometimes these benefit and price differences are used to support market segmentation. A value proposition map shows the relationship between perceived benefit and price of a product. An illustration of this type of relationship is shown in the right hand diagram in Figure 6, where perceived benefit increases, the price increases.

The solid line in the value proposition map shows the benefit/price combinations that are judged by buyers to provide the same value-for-money. A product with three variants offering benefits a, b and c at the shown prices on the indifference curve have the same value-for-money. A product with benefit/price combination placed to the right and below this curve is preferred to any on the curve. The converse also applies, where benefit/price combination placed to the left and above this curve would offer inferior value-for-money to any combination on the curve.

The impact of a change in the benefits on demand is determined by the price elasticity of demand and the inverse of the price elasticity for the benefits. The price elasticity for benefits is calculated from the indifference curve in the value proposition map. The left hand diagram in Figure 6 also shows a broken dashed line that represents the demand corresponding to the value-for-money indifference curve in the value proposition map.

Figure 6 *The relationship between price, benefit and demand of a product (with constant price elasticity of demand)*

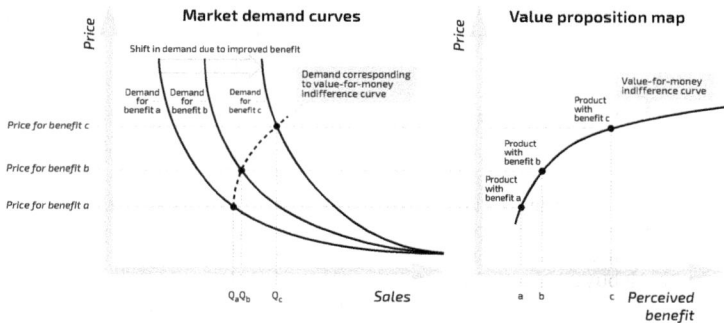

The interplay between a business's price elasticity of demand and benefit elasticity of demand is used to inform appropriate competitive responses, and the response differs whether the business is the cost leader or not. Where the business is not the cost leader, then faced with high price elasticity of demand, the response is to maintain price parity and focus on creating higher value-for-money to gain market share. Recall that high price elasticity of demand is associated with weak product differentiation and more competition. The higher the price elasticity of demand, the stronger the signalling of benefit differences is needed, for example in the form of product design, strong branding, and use of means to associate attributes of luxury and technological leadership with the product. In contrast, where the price elasticity of demand is low (that is strong product differentiation in the market with less competition) then a business can charge a price premium where value-for money is higher than that provided by competing alternatives.

Where the business has lower costs than competitors, focus is on increasing market share by creating further cost reductions through positive cost feedback effects. Other responses depend on the relative magnitude of the price and benefit elasticities of demand. Where the benefit elasticity of demand is greater than the price elasticity of demand, it is more profitable to increase benefit than to reduce price, and vice versa. The competitive responses available to the business include where there are:

- Low price and low benefit elasticities of demand, then maintain price parity with competitors and focus on growing profit margins.
- Low price and high benefit elasticities of demand, then maintain price parity with competitors for comparable products and populate the indifference curve with a range of different benefit/high price products.
- High price and low benefit elasticities of demand, then use price reductions to gain market share.
- High price and high benefit elasticities of demand, then use price reductions and benefit increases to shift the value-for-money indifference curve to the right.

The conclusion to be drawn from this discussion on product differentiation is that detailed understanding of the market and demand is required for pricing, product design and positioning, and competitive strategy. The analysis of data on competitor market share, the perceived benefit and pricing of competing products, and complements, requires techniques to separately estimate price elasticity of demand, price benefit of demand and market structure. Other important considerations are the price of substitutes and complements. Where this analysis involves the lapse of time, income effects also need to be taken into account.

Allocation of value added between competitors

Where the price is set on the continuum between the minimum and maximum value capture thresholds is determined by a business's bargaining power. The mechanism for the allocation of value added between competitors is illustrated by considering a value network consisting of two customers and two providers, in a competitive market, where the providers can individually meet the volume demanded by both buyers, further assume that the cost structures of the providers are the same and do not fall with volume, and say the value added of the product is P_B to each buyer, with providers supplying P_A of value added.

With one unit of the product being purchased by each buyer, then $2P_B$ of value added is created by the value network. The maximum value added available from a buyer to the provider is P_B. The minimum available to a provider is P_A – the cost of production. The maximum value added to be allocated between provider and buyer is (P_B-P_A) because there is no way for a provider to improve their position, as a buyer will simply buy from the other provider. While the maximum value added available to the provider for allocation is P_B from the buyer, because the provider has no bargaining power the buyer captures the surplus value added of $(P_B - P_A)$.

If one of the providers were more efficient than the other, their minimum value added allocated would be set by the next best alternative available to the buyer, which would be to buy from the competitor. The efficient provider would keep the value added as a result of superior performance. Any factor that changes the bargaining power of a provider, such as constraints on the capacity to meet buyer needs, will increase the share of value added captured by a provider.

The drive for super profits from a market disruption

What gives a business strong bargaining power can be understood using the extreme condition of a market-disrupting product. A market disruption is a buyer experience in which the comparative value-for-money increases rapidly and is large enough to be noteworthy. Being noteworthy, buyers are forced to react by re-evaluating their spending patterns in favour of the party disrupting the market. This can apply in any of the element markets in which a business operates. A business, in disrupting the market aims to earn at least for a period of time, a super profit that is more than that achievable by competitors. This super profit is the increase in value added captured from the value network, and its source is from strong bargaining power or lower cost structure that the provider is able to achieve, compared to the other alternatives available to the buyer.

There are three parts to assessing the ability to increase the share of value added by disrupting a market: the magnitude of increase in value-for-money, the comparative bargaining power of the provider, and the strength of the barriers to entry that could act to impede the entry of competitors. A business angle holds the potential to disrupt the market where it offers significantly better value-for-money than alternatives; its bargaining power is high because there are no competitors able to provide a better alternative; and there are high barriers to entry, for example, because it is difficult to copy innovations, the presence of strong brand loyalty, and positive feedback effects.

The ability to extract super profits by disrupting a market is limited where low barriers to entry exist because: the cost difference between providers on entry is low; there are no or weak positive feedback effects; and there are constraints on capacity that limit the maximum size of businesses. In the absence of any other changes in the value network, such as competitor response, a business is able to increase the share of value added captured by adjusting:

- The value of the business by supplying products whose value-for-money is greater than alternatives, for example through product design and market segmentation (Contributor 1). This may be associated with re-positioning the value network.
- The value of the business by selecting and purchasing a set of inputs to support a highly productive production process (Contributor 2), for example in the choice of employment contracts.
- The productivity and cost structure of the production process to turn core competencies into valuable assets (Contributor 3). This includes the choice of activity type and organisational structure to achieve this.
- The reliability of the business to deliver on business plans and the resilience to realise on-going profitability (Contributor 4), for example by using insurance and currency forward contracts.
- The value of the business through financial management (Contributor 5), for example by the use of capital gearing.

Scarce resources can be developed and applied in each of the element markets.

The impacts of a market disruption

For an existing product with an established demand, a market disruption can increase the quantity demanded for a product because it offers increased value-for-money. Diagrammatically this is shown by a move along the supply curve. Figure 7 shows a scenario where a legacy supply curve is supplanted by a new supply curve. This new supply curve is a much lower price cost using highly scalable systems and processes. Lower cost of supply results in total quantity demand increasing from Q_1 to Q_2.

Figure 7 also shows the impact, where the new supply curve changes the taste for a product as a result of familiarity and experience of learning about its benefits through consumption. This is a secondary effect of the market disruption, in that the demand curve is shifted to the right and the total quantity demand increases from Q_2 to Q_3. This learning effect can operate rapidly. Where a completely new product is taken to market, learning by consuming is a significant mechanism through which demand is established. This mechanism is also able to explain why some products fail when taken to market yet others succeed. The difference is the degree to which the product design and launch strategy is able to stimulate demand through familiarity and learning by consuming, which itself requires behavioural change on the part of buyers and social network feedback effects.

The observation from this is that market disruption has greatest impact where the market (Q_1) is large. If initial market share is gained from legacy suppliers, where the price elasticity of demand is high, then an increase in market size is anticipated from a reduction in value-for-money (shown here by a reduction in price and resultant increase in market share ($Q_2 - Q_1$)), and an increase in market size from growth due to buyer behaviour change ($Q_3 - Q_2$) brought about by a significant increase in value-for-money.

Figure 7 *Change in supply curve as a result of a significant disruption in the market, and a shift in the demand curve from an increased demand for the product from learning by consuming the product*

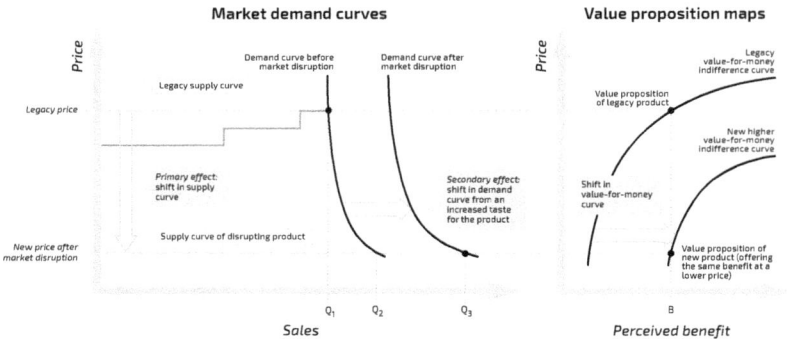

Social and temporal effects

Some factors that influence demand have a simple (even if it is unpredictable) effect on demand. Examples of these factors are state of the economy, cultural norms, brand loyalty, fads and zeitgeist. The influence is simple because on their own these factors do not exhibit feedback effects. Feedback reinforces any change so that change causes further change. Where the feedback is positive, the change is reinforced and results in increased demand. Feedback can also be negative, and any change can result in reduced demand. Feedback impacts on demand are provided by bandwagon and social network effects.

The bandwagon effect refers to the attractiveness of being part of the same group at a stage in the value network. The bandwagon effect indicates a positive relationship in which attractiveness increases with increasing membership, but this relationship could also be negative, at least for some people. A telephone network is of greater usefulness, the more people are connected to it. The more people who can be telephoned, the more people will want to subscribe to it. Telephone networks have a strong positive bandwagon effect. Identifying the group of users with common interests who want to be connected is required to activate the bandwagon effect. Community interest groups can also exhibit positive bandwagon effect and are more attractive where they cater for specific interests. Cities also display strong positive bandwagon effect, but this is limited by externalities, for instance by transport congestion. Bandwagon effect is negative where, for example, increased membership leads to congestion and lock-in.

The bandwagon effect from the attractiveness of being part of the same group is different from declining cost economies, in which average cost falls with an increase in the number of users and use. Simply put, the bandwagon effect is a demand-side phenomenon, whereas scale effect operates on the supply-side. Communications, transport and logistics networks are scale-free infrastructure networks, and have strong scale effects from falling average costs with more dense groups of users. Another demand-side phenomenon occurs because of referrals from others, such as through social networks. These social network 'contagions' lead to increased demand occuring between connected agents in a group, such as who can be buyers, sellers, finance providers, and friends. In some instances positive feedback effects are so significant that they can dominate business success in the form of fads. In reality it is a matter of luck, not size of value-for-money, which determines what product gets adopted through strong positive buyer reaction. Aside from the benefits to buyers, which can come from standardisation of product choice from widespread adoption of a product, strong social preferences can also impose limits. This occurs where it inhibits innovation of better solutions and locks buyers into particular solutions or suppliers.

Summary

Businesses operate in at least five different element markets. Each element market provides a potential contributor to value. A business creates FCF value by providing buyers with products of greater value-for-money than available from alternatives (Contributor 1). This may be associated with re-positioning the value network. It is also able to create value by selecting a set of inputs to support a high productivity production process and through economical purchase of those inputs (Contributor 2). In addition, a business creates FCF value by operating a highly productive production process and delivering planned outputs (Contributor 3). FCF value is improved by the use of risk mitigants, to ensure that business plans are met, and strategic options, to provide the capacity to respond to changes in market context (Contributor 4). Business value is enhanced by financial management to provide the best use of resources in the face of changes in value and deviations between the different values brought about by changes in business performance and market context (Contributor 5).

Segmenting and combining market segments, present businesses with opportunities to capture a share of value added. Segments can be created in a number of ways, for example through product design, pricing and perceived benefit, barriers to access, availability of substitutes and links to complements, and brand. In extreme situations businesses can deliberately disrupt existing market structure. A market disruption is a buyer experience where the comparative value-for-money increases rapidly and is large enough to be noteworthy. Being noteworthy, the buyer is forced to react by re-evaluating their spending patterns in favour of the party disrupting the market. This can apply in any of the element markets a business operates in. By disrupting the market a business aims to earn, at least for a period of time, a super profit that is more than that achievable by competitors. In each of the element markets scarce resources can be developed and applied.

Selected literature review

Early origin of idea

The demand curve is a well-established concept, having being first introduced in 1890 by Alfred Marshall in his book *Principles of Economics,* and is explained in textbooks on business economics.

The early champion of the importance of disrupting the established allocation of value added in a market through the hunt for, and pursuit of, business opportunities was the economist Joseph Schumpeter; described in *Capitalism, Socialism and Democracy* which appeared in 1942. He envisaged that through a process of active participation in markets businesspeople create new opportunities for themselves and, in doing so, undermine the business models used by incumbents. This process of creative destruction involves finding new market-disrupting business angles. An opportunity can arise in a number of ways, for example by changing the value-for-money of products and assets to buyers, through more efficient production processes, more economical acquisition of inputs or the better management of risk (the knowable component of uncertainty). To Schumpeter, participants in the market who cannot make the investment to at least copy the successful, fall by the wayside.

Key influences on the work

The explanation of the allocation of value added between the parties in a value network is described by Bowman and Ambrosini in a 2000 article 'Value Creation Versus Value Capture: Towards a Coherent Definition of Value in Strategy' published in *British Journal of Management.* The buyers' point of reference in value capture by the business is set out by the 2007 paper 'A consumer perspective on value creation' by Priem in a 2007 edition of *The Academy of Management Review.*

THREE
The entire value network matters

The importance of understanding the entire value network to the ability to capture value is vividly chronicled in the history of the spice trade, particularly the changes that occurred in the middle ages. With the conquest of the Byzantine Empire in 1453, the Ottoman Empire gained control over the Western European spice trade levying heavy taxes on goods destined for Western Europe. One response to this was the push to discover alternative trade routes to circumvent the Ottoman Empire. In 1497 the Portuguese navigator Vasco da Gama succeeded in rounding the Cape of Good Hope and reaching the Indian sub-continent. The Portuguese then successfully developed this route, becoming the commercial centre of the Western European spice trade. Political changes in Europe from the amalgamation of the Spanish and Portuguese thrones, Dutch wars of independence from Spain and animosity between Spain and England, spurred the English and Dutch to enter the spice trade in 1591 and 1595, respectively. The Dutch effectively replaced the Portuguese by the late 1600's, and then set about trying to gain control of the south east Asia islands where cloves and nutmeg are indigenous. This attempt was thwarted by competitors who were able to transplant seedlings and grow them in new territories. This act dramatically changed the nature of the spice trade. This was the real market disruption to the spice trade as now these spices could be sourced from many different places at low price. What started as an attempt by the Ottoman Empire to increase their share of the value added, resulted in the complete remodelling of the spice value network and making spices much cheaper to consumers.

Introduction

Businesses operate within a wide web of business activities, all of which contribute to the delivery of products. The form and function of the participants in this value network are pliable, with flexibility in products offered and capabilities undertaken within businesses - even though the pliability of a business is limited once it has invested in its capabilities. The clusters of capabilities that constitute a value network differ from one another and are in constant change. This chapter explains the setting of the business in the wider network of business angles presented by others, and that the business angle is malleable, able to be crafted to pursue perceived opportunities by changing its products and capabilities. This matters because the objective of business is to extract a share of the value added available within a value network, where choice of business angle is the instrument to achieve this.

The approach followed in this chapter is to describe some of the factors that shape the boundaries and structure of the value network. The key determinant of the boundaries between stages in a value network is transaction costs. Most value networks support a range of intermediary markets and a final market. However, there is a class of value network where this is not the case, here instead it provides a platform through which at least two different groups are able to transact. The allocation of value added between the parties participating in a value network is determined by bargaining power, and this is also discussed.

Organisational boundaries and the structure of the value network

Value network

A value network is the cluster of capabilities that culminate in the capacity to deliver products to buyers. In this way value networks create value added. A value network can consist of distinct clusters of businesses that compete with other clusters. This is not a neat separation of a value network into different stages, with each business in a stage having the same capability and capacity as other businesses in that stage. Indeed, it is easily apparent that this is not the case, moreover, some businesses contribute to several clusters and these can be in different value networks. Nonetheless, some members of a cluster can be tightly bound together in buyer-supplier relationships with relationship specific investment, or through strong positive feedback effects making it difficult to switch out of the relationship.

A business joins a cluster that provides it with the best share of the value added created by the value network. A cluster provides the best allocation of value added for its members. A business leaves a cluster if there is another cluster able to provide a better share of the available value added, similarly a cluster will replace a business with a new one if this increases the value added available to the other members. The coalitions of businesses in a cluster operate in consort, even if this is not a formal relationship. Clusters compete with other clusters operating in the same value network. A node comprises the capabilities to deliver outputs, and operates at one stage in the value network. The collective capability of all nodes in a value network delivers final consumption products. A business consists of one or more of these nodes.

To illustrate this idea, consider the global value network for the training of air traffic controllers. In this market training is provided under contract to Air Navigation Service Providers (ANSPs) for personnel recruited by the ANSP. Services and equipment to support training are provided from specialist suppliers of equipment such as training simulators, and services such as psychological tests. This value network, dominated by national interests, has only two types of suppliers of training: in-house trainers and commercial training providers. Outside of the USA there are, in 2010, a small number of established businesses providing this training. With the use of more sophisticated air traffic control equipment, training simulators are now used which are provided by specialists in this equipment. Training is also expensive, a cost paid by the future employer, and pre-screening of candidates is frequently carried out using psychological tests. The development of these tests is also carried out by specialist suppliers.

The different business angles that contribute to a value network are depicted in the value network map, such as that in Figure 8. This value network map shows that this value network is dominated by ANSPs, which are vertically integrated public sector entities that undertake all elements in the training process of air traffic controllers. There are some ANSPs that do not undertake their own training, but purchase this service from specialist training providers. The diagram also shows that some vertically integrated ANSPs also contract out some training, mainly as a way to acquire overflow capacity. A component to providing training is access to suitable training technology, especially training simulators that simulate the air traffic control environment at specific airports. The specialist nature of this technology means in most instances it is purchased from businesses that specialise in the development of this type of equipment. While provision of this equipment is increasingly from specialist suppliers, some ANSPs, although a diminishing number, continue to build some specialist support equipment in-house.

Figure 8 *High level value network map showing market share and types of participants in the provision of trained air traffic controllers (2010)*

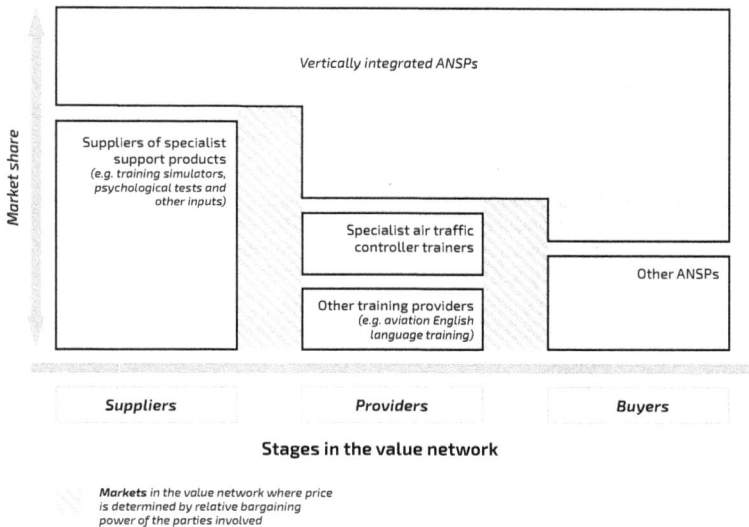

Markets in the value network where price
is determined by relative bargaining
power of the parties involved

The implications of the characterisation of businesses as members of a value network are, that: on the one hand, clusters compete with other clusters in the same markets; while on the other hand, clusters are changed and reconfigured as market context changes. The prime driver for reforming the clusters is the relentless drive by each party in a value network to increase their share of the available value added. The opportunity to increase the expected share of value added is enough to drive a party to leave one cluster and join another.

One of the ramifications of this is that each business is out to manipulate the value network to its own ends with the aim of appropriating value added. This includes behaving in a way that is not totally in the best interests of its buyers. The opportunity for agency problems is most prevalent where high transaction costs exist.

Characterisation of the value network by its markets

The value network map also shows that competitive markets exist between the stages in the value network. Demand and supply factors determine the allocation of value added at these points. It is these exchanges between the stages in the value network where allocation of value added between the various participants takes place. To draw an analogy using the harvesting of energy in water as hydroelectricity and the flow of water through a river system, the value network equates to the river system, the nodes and stages are the barrages that dam and divert the water, and markets are the hydro-generation facilities. It is the flow that is important to understand, as these are the products in the market. Demand and supply graphs are used to show these flows. The nodes are where value is created through core competencies.

Products are the embodiment of the transaction between the capabilities in the network. Products are endorsed through repeat transactions, and in that way they are the currency through which opportunities are exploited and value captured by businesses. As the embodiment of the transaction, a product plays the role of the talisman on which to focus actions to increase their value-for-money. The path of the outplaying of the process of creative destruction in the market is signposted by products. Products are also the link between the different components or nodes in the value network and allocate value to each node. Products are also complex. There are three different types of products:

- **Exchange products** provide a high degree of readiness for use, through for example, custom, standardisation and specification, and transfer decision-making rights to consume or use to the buyer on sale, if not entirely, then at least for a period of time.
- **Interface products** are associated with the interaction with systems and processes, or channels for delivering exchange products. Frequently, interface products reduce transaction costs and increase access. Interface products are sometimes bundled with an exchange product and may not be offered as stand-alone product offerings.
- **Applications products** extend the use of knowhow, systems and processes to new adjacent workflow processes or value networks by providing additional functionality. In addition to the application specific functionality, application products utilise at least one exchange (which incorporates at least one interface product).

There may be opportunities for the supply of each of these product types. In other instances, the product types can be combined. Products are monetised through these different ways. Two-part pricing used by network utilities is an example of the bundling and separate charging for an exchange product and interface product (the connection to the network). The freemium product model frequently involves the bundling of a free interface product with high price/value-for-money interface and application products.

This definition of product is derived from its role in the value network. Products have a range of attributes that can include tangible, intangible, service and ceremony components. Musical instruments, sheet music and music recording devices and players are tangible, music is intangible; and the performance and distribution of musical works have service and ceremony components. Products also have attributes of product meaning derived from the social, cultural and institutional setting.

Complex value networks

Most businesses operate a single activity type, producing a range of products that provide revenue from mainly similar market segments. Even complex businesses are analysed as a collection of single activity types servicing mainly similar market segments. This statement holds true even where the business produces more than one product type, which can be co-products, by-products and waste products. These secondary products owe their existence to the production processes and lifecycle of the primary product. Here the value network is still linear in acquiring inputs to be transformed into one or more outputs, which fork out from the main transformation activity.

A business's products can participate in a number of value networks, each of which may require separate analysis. The training of air traffic controllers is a simple example of a value network. More often the value network is complex and fragmented, in the sense of comprising many different businesses of different sizes. The relationships between the capabilities of different businesses in a value network can be complex because several different products are involved and need to be coordinated, both at a point in time and place, and sometimes over long periods of time. The delivery of products can also involve several businesses. Returning to the example of air traffic controller training, that value network is one of many contributors to the ANSP value network. There are other input value networks into the ANSP value network, such as the provision of air navigation systems for which a separate value network could be drawn.

Over time, the complexity of the structure of value networks, and the attributes of products exchanged between stages within the value network, and between different value networks that a business is engaged with, changes and reconfigure in response to changes in market context. These changes have been significant in recent decades in the application of information and communications technology (ICT) to logistics. Opportunities have emerged that have enabled truck transport operators to develop from being a commodity supplier of capacity to highly coordinated just-in-time logistics providers integral to the coordinated delivery of items from suppliers to their customers. This is a key component, for instance, of supermarket operations.

Businesses participate in at least five element markets, and participation is in at least one value network in each of these markets. For most businesses it is not meaningful to develop value network maps for markets other than the product market, because they are such small operators in these other markets. They are price takers in these other markets and no useful information is gained by analysis of them. Where it is appropriate, a separate value network map is generated for each market in which the business is a participant.

Positive feedback effects

Also impacting on the complexity of a value network are cross-product effects. When the relationship is positive the products are complementary, and when negative they are substitutes. Cross-product effects can also be indirect, for example, the availability of parcel pickup lockers at a supermarket increases its sale of other products. The existence of cross-product effects cause other value networks to come into, or go out of, existence. The cross-product effect is a demand-side phenomenon, which is different from by-, co- and waste products created in the production process.

Another related effect is between groups of products. Supermarkets and department stores exhibit strong positive cross-product effects whereby the greater range of products (and suppliers) attracts more buyers. In turn, a greater number of buyers attracts more suppliers to want to have their products stocked by the store.

The phenomenon, where the demand for a product is influenced by demand by another group of buyers or users is the cross-group effect. Cross-group effects can also be positive or negative. The impacts of strong positive cross-group effects on a value network are twofold. A boundary occurs in the value network at the point where the cross-group effect takes place, breaking it into two stages with industry consolidation occurring in either or both stages. Their existence also creates a business opportunity to provide a platform to facilitate transactions from which cross-group effects are created. These platforms are the production process supplied by a multi-sided platform provider, which enables at least two parties to transact directly with one another, and are discussed in detail below.

Determinant of the boundary between businesses

Transaction costs

Why value networks break up at particular points into stages - the boundaries of businesses - is determined by transaction costs. For the calculation of transaction costs the entire purchase through to delivery cycle is taken into account. Transaction costs include the costs associated with locating a party. This includes the cost of making a second best choice because the first best party could not be located, for instance, in buyers trying to locate suppliers, as well as all costs incurred from the time of the desire to commence a transaction through to its satisfactory conclusion. The explanation for this is that efficiency is maximised by aligning transactions (which have differing attributes and institutional arrangements) with the organisational structure within businesses (which have different attributes and costs).

Transactions differ in: frequency, certainty, specificity of the transaction, and ease of measurement of performance in delivering products to the agreed specification. Specificity is the ability to describe the product required. Some products require investment to be made by the supplier in the transaction. This investment is highly transaction specific where the asset involved cannot be redeployed to alternative uses or users without loss of value. For example, a supplier may need to develop software, which has no other use, to meet the buyer's requirements. Asset specificity is significant because, when it is low, the procurement of products on the open market has an advantage over owning the capabilities to produce them. Generally speaking, when many businesses are competing to provide a product of similar specification, the market-place provides stronger incentives for performance than could be placed on an internal supplier. When asset specificity is high, or there are very few alternative uses of the capabilities, managing the work internally by owning the capability, is the preferred management form. Markets do not function well where there is no competition to provide incentives for performance, and a high degree of dependency can develop between the buyer and supplier. When asset specificity is intermediate, hybrid forms of management, such as long-term contracts or franchise relationships with appropriate incentives and sanctions, are the preferred management form.

Coordination between different stages in a value network

At this point it is worth commenting on the different types of coordination that can occur between stages in a value network. Many consumer products involve the supplier manufacturing the product as a precursor to offering them for sale. But this is only one of the four ways businesses interact. Push/pull involves the production for inventory to support, for instance, on-demand delivery to the buyer. Push/push is where the quantity supplied is determined by the volume produced and the coordination problem is solved by pricing. This occurs, for example, in the processing of perishable produce supplied to markets. Pull/push provides access to on-demand production typically for consolidation with other products before delivery to the buyer. Pull/pull relates to on-demand production. These different ways of buyers and suppliers coordinating their transactions impact transaction costs. ICT and integrated logistics systems have dramatically removed transaction costs in pull/pull coordination, which has reduced the need for inventories in some settings. This is just-in-time coordination.

Regulatory and institutional arrangements

Regulatory and institutional arrangements that impact on barriers to entry, access to alternatives, and profitability in a market, also influence the shape of a value network. Anti-competitive legislation restricts consolidation and business practices, such as collusion, where groups of buyers or providers agree terms and conditions beneficial to themselves, which are judged to be to the detriment to the rest of society.

Changes in transaction costs flow through the value network

The entire value network is redesigned by changing transaction costs, including the products and the coordination between stages. The shape of the value network and its division into clusters and businesses reflect transaction costs. The boundary of the clusters is also reflected in the products interchanged and the demand relationship at each stage. As an example of this, the adoption of a standardised shipping container reduced the transaction costs between freight forwarders and shippers. It heralded a complete redesign of long distance logistics (covering ships, handling equipment, storage facilities, rail rolling stock and trucks), creating a new more efficient value network.

The consequence of reduced transaction costs is increased fragmentation in a value network. The existence of these differences is used as an arbitrage opportunity to create new business opportunities. An element of innovation in the business angle, is creating a place at a particular point in a value network by removing transaction costs.

Multi-sided platforms

Multi-sided markets

The relationship between the participants in a value network can take two forms: a buyer-supplier relationship, and a multi-sided platform (MSP) relationship. The essential feature of an MSP is that it enables two or more groups to transact directly with one another. This is done by providing the platform for interchanges between various groups, but not actually taking part in the contractual relationship between parties. The key features of MSPs are illustrated by the various platforms that enable buyers to locate potential suppliers. Examples of platforms that do this are the postal service, advertising supported media and introduction agents such as job boards. An MSP consists of a platform provider and at least two groups of users (generically referred to as senders and receivers) who transact directly with one another through the facilities of the platform. An MSP is a particular way of intermediating in a value network. In single-sided markets suppliers deal directly with buyers with no involvement from an intermediary, that is in a buyer-supplier relationship. Where the relationship between suppliers and buyers is through an intermediary, such as a reseller, the direct customer relationship with the buyer is held by the reseller and not the supplier. As for resellers, an MSP facilitates buyers acquiring products from suppliers, but unlike resellers they enable buyers to directly deal with suppliers.

An MSP is a class of value network, where products are provided to at least two quite different markets (one for each group), but equally, success in one market influences success in the other market. Here the value network, in addition to an input acquisition method, utilises at least two delivery methods to deliver different outputs that are related through cross-group effects operating between the two user groups. The postal service is an example of this. The postal service inserts itself in the value network between senders and receivers, two different groups of users with different demand characteristics, with the objective of removing shared transaction cost. Figure 9 provides an illustration of the postal service value network map with its two groups of users. The diagram also shows direct marketing services, a value adding service provided to enable merchants to use the mail communications to advertise their products. Note the C-shape of the value network with senders and receivers at the two end points that is characteristic of an MSP.

Figure 9 *High level value network map showing market share and key participants in the provision of (monopoly) postal services*

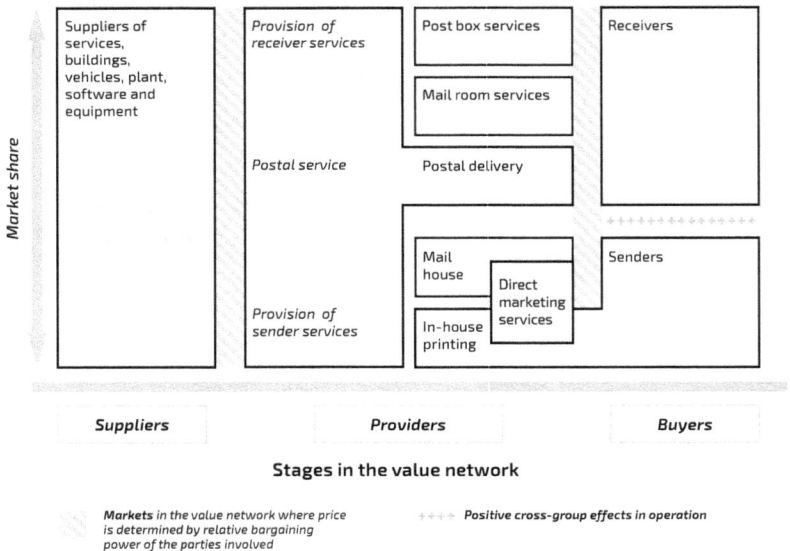

Markets in the value network where price is determined by relative bargaining power of the parties involved

Positive cross-group effects in operation

The cross-group effects in an MSP are negative, neutral or positive. Gift and donations registers (such as an organ and tissue donation register) are examples of MSPs with no cross-group feedback. Negative feedback effects occur in media (print, radio, television and web) where there is strong reaction to too much advertising. As might be expected with cross-group interactions there are no universal rules. While negative feedback effects occur widely in media they are not universal. There are examples where the media channel achieves the position of a fashion trade directory, in which case, the more high quality high fashion advertisements there are in an issue, the more attractive it is to a greater number of fashion conscious readers.

Cross-group price effects

Not all MSPs are operated by commercial organisations. Some are made available to participating groups with limited conditions on usage, for example some open source software. A variety of pricing models have been developed for commercial platforms. A common model is to charge the party who gains most monetary benefit from access to the platform, and to make access to the other parties using the platform free, or at a low price, in order to drive usage.

Differences in benefit to the various parties to an MSP are most easily seen where there are strong positive cross-group effects. This is illustrated by the postal service, where in the presence of strong cross-group feedback from having the entire population connected to the platform, there is a shift in the demand curve for significant senders wanting to access the reach offered by the platform. In this situation, the loss of revenue from making mail ostensibly free to receivers is more than compensated by the increased revenue from significant senders who wish to reach large numbers of receivers. The demand curve for receivers is highly sensitive to price. Few may pay to receive letters, as bills are the single most common letter. On the other hand the number of senders is sensitive to reach, with the demand curve shifting to the right as reach increases. With appropriate elasticities, the loss in revenue from making access to the postal network free to receivers is more than compensated by the increase in revenue from senders, from the increased reach of the network. When cross-group effects are taken into account, receivers are key customers of the platform as they provide reach, whose value is extracted from senders because of cross-group effects.

This relationship between the shifts in the demand curve faced by senders, as a result of more receivers on the platform, keeping price constant, is shown in the left-hand diagram in Figure 10. An alternative representation of this relationship between the number of receivers and number of senders, keeping price constant, is given in the right-hand diagram. The shape of this curve shows that the platform is increasingly attractive to senders as more receivers join. More complex preferences may exist where there are more than two parties interacting with one another.

Figure 10 *Depiction of the relationship of demand from senders for different levels of access to receivers as demand curves and participation curve*

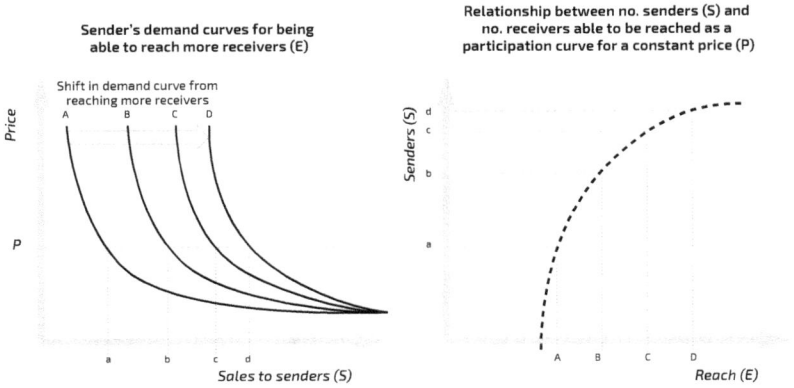

The cross-group interactions that operate in a two-sided market can be depicted in a single diagram. Continuing with the mail example, the two groups of users are senders (S) and receivers (R). In these markets: access to content (C) drives the number of receivers; and access to delivery that reaches receivers (E) drives the number of senders. The key to depicting the participation curves for senders and receivers is to express the two relationships in common variables. This is done by equating content to the number of senders, and delivery reach to the number of receivers. A depiction of the construction of participation curves showing a two-sided market relationship between receivers and senders (assuming constant prices) in a single diagram (bottom right hand corner) is set out in Figure 11.

Figure 11 *Depiction of the construction of participation curves showing a two-sided market relationship between senders and receivers (at constant price)*

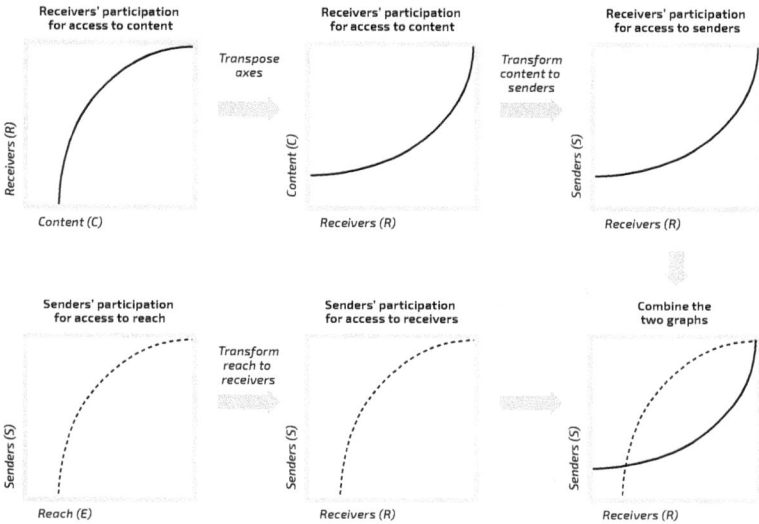

This representation of cross-group interaction in a two-sided market is useful in analysing some of the critical features of MSPs with positive cross-group effects (MSP+s) because it shows how changes on one side of the market impact on the other sides of the market. The arrows in Figure 12 show the compound direction of these feedback effects. For example, if the starting point was S_1 number of senders, then they would like R_S number of receivers on the platform. With S_1 number of senders, R_R number of receivers would be interested in joining the platform. Where senders' participation for reach (R_S) is more than receivers' participation to access content (R_R) then the absence of positive feedback effects will cause participation to collapse to the origin (bottom left hand corner). The resultant value network is that for a single-sided market. This situation occurs where one or both value propositions are weak (the two curves do not intersect) or, where they do, critical mass has not been achieved. The vast majority of potential MSP+s fail because of these two factors. For those few cases where the value proposition to both sides of the market are sufficiently strong to cause an overlap in the two curves, then positive feedback effects operate to propel, in the absence of competitive alternatives, the product to the maximum participation point. This can be very strong and the journey very rapid. MSPs are valuable because of the market size that these cross-group feedback effects can open up.

The groups in MSPs with strong positive cross-group effects have different variables that influence their behaviour. All of the multiple sides of the market must have cross-group effects. The participation curves for each side of the market must intersect. A stronger overlap in the participation curves pulls the critical mass point towards the origin making the launch of the platform easier. Once critical mass is achieved, positive feedback effects can rapidly pull market share up to the maximum participation point. Failure to achieve critical mass confines a business to operating in a single-sided market.

That each group has different variables influencing their behaviour means the task of stimulating and maintaining cross-group effects is complex with value propositions. Marketing and sales initiatives need to be tailored to each group. It also provides the possibility of using variables in such a way to derive a behavioural response in one group, whose benefit can be harvested in the other group. Making use of the platform free to receivers can drive adoption by that group, increases its value to senders, and revenue is taken by charging senders who are less sensitive to price.

Figure 12 *Participation curves showing the operation of low and high value propositions, and positive cross-group effects with the resulting force (shown by direction of solid arrows)*

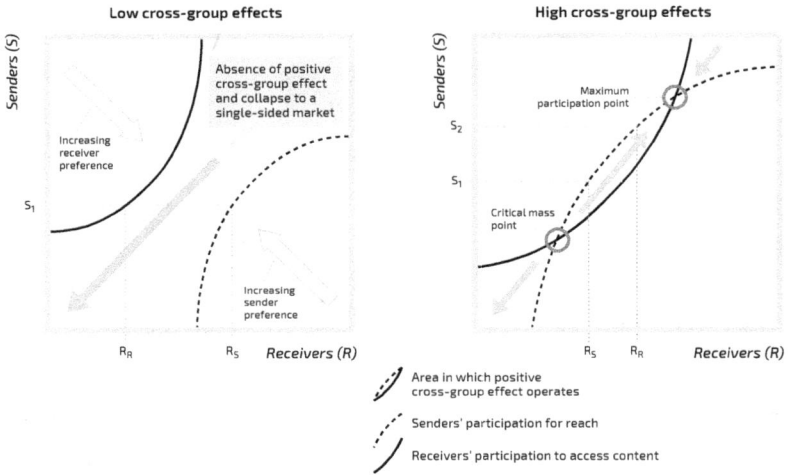

How the platform operator makes profit and the consequences of this

The aim of participants in value networks is to increase their value added, by increasing the share of the value added within the value network (grow the size of their slice of the pie), and that available in a market (grow the size of the pie). This applies also to MSP+s, where the platform operator has the additional challenge of influencing cross-group effects so as to increase the total value added to all users. The platform operator, however, wants to do this in such a way so as to increase the value added they are able to capture by removing shared transaction costs between the groups of users. Removal of shared transaction costs is the essence of why MSPs exist. The payback from stimulating strong positive cross-group effects is a rapid increase in market share driven by positive feedback effects.

The introduction of an MSP has other consequences. By lowering transaction costs, MSPs change the boundaries of capabilities in the value network in which it participates, and introduces new products and markets. Removing transaction costs introduces new exchange and interface products that can also introduce new methods of coordination. These in turn can create opportunities for suppliers of applications products.

The risk faced by MSPs is that users and competitors bypass the platform. This threat of disintermediation is one of the strong motivations for platform providers to continually increase the value added by the platform to users. The impact of attrition in the participation curves on a two-sided market is illustrated in Figure 13. The diagram shows two situations: a reduction in receiver preference for the platform (shift to the left of the receiver participation curve); and a reduction in the value-for-money of the platform due to competing offers (shift to the right of the sender participation curve). The net impact of these two changes is for the point of maximum participation to move to the point labelled 'new position'. With sufficient loss in value to users, the two curves part and no longer overlap, the positive feedback effects are lost and the market will collapse to a single-sided market. It is also worth noting in this illustration that the impact of a loss in value to the user is different for the two preference functions. On its own, a reduction in sender preference because of a reduction in value-for-money, say from a price increase, is less than the loss in value because of a reduction in the preference to use by the receiver. MSPs are highly vulnerable to disintermediation. Pricing on one side of the market could have a disproportionate impact on other groups of users – pricing matters in MSPs.

The existence of cross-group effects says nothing about the effects of competition – either in terms of the ability to retain customers (stickiness) or the ability of multiple competitors to coexist in the market.

Figure 13 *Illustration of some changes in the sender and receiver participation curves*

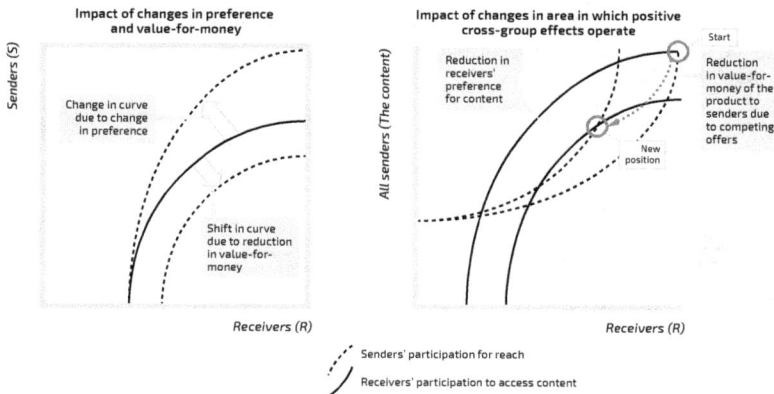

Market size and the premium for uncertainty

The outstanding fact in the creation of valuable MSPs is the need to solve the chicken-and-egg problem of getting enough parties on to the platform in order to achieve critical mass. Launch is a severe problem for potential MSP+s platform providers, with the vast majority of initiatives failing, including those by businesses with huge resources. The ability to create an MSP+ carries a high degree of uncertainty.

The three stages in the early market uptake of an MSP+ are depicted in the right hand diagram in Figure 14. The three stages are: a launch stage characterised by relatively slow growth that is proportional to marketing effort. This is followed by an explosive growth stage where critical mass is achieved and positive feedback effects propel uptake. The rate of this growth is related to the size of the overlap between the participation curves. In the final stage the rate of growth slows. The market uptake rate slows because the point of maximum participation is being approached, and/or the end of product lifecycle is setting in, and/or rivalry from a competing offer reduces market share. The market uptake trajectory from this point on will depend on which of these reasons is applicable. Figure 14 also shows the relationship between the stylised market uptake trajectory and the diagram of participation in a two-sided platform. In this depiction the participation curve diagram is rotated 45° counter clockwise. The vertical axis shows a simplified growth path from launch, passing through the critical mass point and on through to point of maximum participation.

For existing products, market analysis can establish the point of maximum participation. For an entirely new proposition, it is impossible to assess the potential market uptake beforehand. For this, a market launch is required, supported by mechanisms to gather information on user experience in order to evaluate and improve the value proposition. The launch stage requires active marketing and sales effort, and resources have to be applied to "push the cart up the hill" to the point where critical mass is achieved and explosive growth commences. An indicator of whether positive feedback effects have begun in the market uptake stages is the rate of customer usage for market acquisition effort – for example as measured by the return on marketing investment (ROMI).

Figure 14 *Stages in the early market uptake of an MSP+ and the relationship to the two-sided platform participation curves*

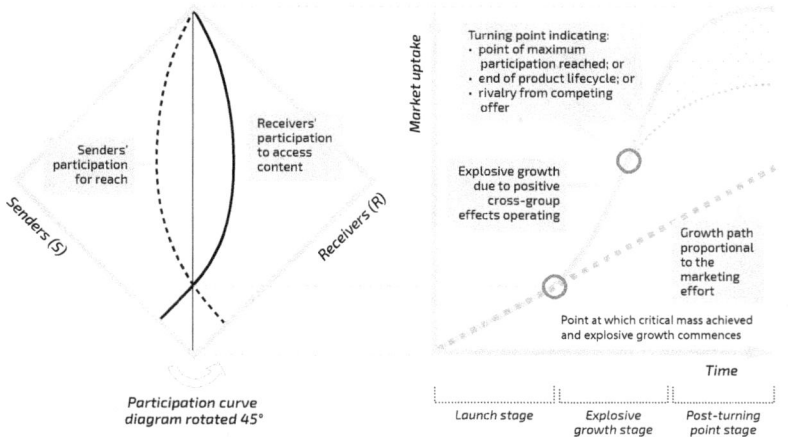

The attainment of critical mass is also dependent on market size and the competitive alternatives available. The market opportunity in a small market requires the participation curves to be enhanced so that the point of critical mass is shifted towards the origin and within the available market size. MSP+s can operate at a local level, such as market places, shopping malls and local newspapers. In small markets the success of platforms is critically dependent on designing highly valuable propositions for all parties to the platform in the target markets. The strength of the positive feedback effects is influenced by the strength of the valuable propositions to all parties to the platform. The stronger the value propositions and their promotion, the greater the gains from positive feedback effects. The difficulty of gaining critical mass in a small market also means that the market is likely to be less concentrated, with a poorer level of service to users. From this discussion it is concluded that two key features contribute to an increase in the likelihood of gaining critical mass: having high value propositions, and its promotion to all groups of users (large overlap between participation curves); and launching into an existing group of users who value the new offering (to aid overcoming the critical mass point).

Allocation of value added in a value network

Watersheds in the allocation of value added within a value network

Information about the other participants with which a business interrelates is summarised in the value network map. Knowing this contributes to understanding the bargaining power between participants. Demand and supply relationships exist between stages in the value network. The outcome of the bargaining is summarised in the demand and supply relationships. The price struck in a market for a product is determined by the cost structure of suppliers, and the bilateral bargaining power of the parties involved. Bilateral bargaining power is in turn dictated by the strength of the value proposition, the market share of the parties involved, their behaviour, the ability of participants to enter and leave the market, information available to the participants, cross-product and cross-group effects, competitive alternatives, and institutional arrangement.

Impact of changes in other parts of the value network on the ability to capture value

The changes to the demand and supply relationships changes the allocation of value added between the parties in a value network. Factors that can change the relationship include changes in:

- The bargaining power of any party in the value network.
- The value-of-money of competing products.
- The productivity of a supplier or provider.
- Capacity constraints on suppliers and providers, and demand from buyers.
- Transaction costs between parties, for example, the ability of buyers to find suppliers.
- Market structure, the number and size of buyers, competitive alternatives and suppliers.
- Access to resources that are restricted because of intellectual property protection, ownership rights or markets in which to trade these assets.
- Government regulation and institutional arrangements that can influence any of the factors above.

When considered in the context of a value network, these changes are likely to impact the allocation of value in the whole value network and not be localised to a business. As an example, a new entrant into a value network with the lowest average cost, on the one hand, adds capacity lowering the minimum value available for capture, while on the other hand, creates new cluster configuration for existing participants, increasing the share of value added which can be capture by the cluster.

Dynamic drivers of change in the value network

To recap, from the discussion in the previous chapter, associated with a perceived business opportunity is an expected quantum of value added generated by the value network, portions of which are captured by each of the participants in the value network. The value network accounts for the total value added associated with a business opportunity to all participants. Part of this is captured by buyers in the form of perceived benefit, part by providers in the form of profit, and part by suppliers of inputs. Businesspeople and scarce resource owners seek to find ways to share in this value added, and more. This includes the initial resources put up by businesspeople to explore a new opportunity or the losses funded by shareholders and creditors – where regulatory and institutional arrangements allow this. They do this by providing products for sale. This sharing of value added between the participants is the foundation of commerce but is skewed in favour of participants with a source of advantage that strengthens their bargaining power.

Businesses innovate with the objective of increasing profit by changing the allocation of value added in its favour. These profits are derived from innovations in four areas. Innovation in the identity of the target market, the market value proposition, product attributes, and price, and how these compare to alternatives. Innovation can also take place in resource usage, their value to the business and price, and value-for-money achieved from these resources by competitors. The production processes to be used in the acquisition and delivery capabilities, and their productivity and profit expectations are a fruitful area of innovation. Innovation can also take place in the capital requirements and the exposure to loss, and impact on the option premium to businesspeople, as well as the financial management of the businesses resources. Innovation in any of these areas changes which parties capture the value added. Having listed the ways value added is created, it must be quickly acknowledged that success is dependent on dynamic behaviour in the market, which produces uncertainty, and the strength of any positive feedback demand effects, or declining cost economies.

Innovation though the collaboration of several participants in a value network

In addition to occurring in any of the five contributors to value, innovation frequently involves several participants working together to give commercial effect to it. Indeed, the process to create new knowledge, how it is dispersed, and how it is then used depends not only on businesses working together but the wider institutional, commercial and social structure in which businesses operate. Collaboration can be used to create new opportunities, and in this way improve option premiums. Collaboration is also an effective way to reduce and share the cost of uncertainty, particularly where the pace of change is high. However, business behaviour is generally 'to go it alone'. This is despite the fact that internal factors, such as cost and limitations on resourcing, are the main impediments to innovation.

Innovation in the context of the other participants in a value network

Markets undergoing change present opportunities for businesses to find new ways to participate in the value network. With change, all other things being equal, the allocation of the value added between parties in that market changes. This frequently reveals itself in a adjustment in market share. The total value added available can also change. Prices may fall where the resulting network is more economically efficient, both in terms of productivity and allocation of risks to parties most willing to bear them. Where there is a price fall (rise) total demand may increase (decrease). A reallocation of value added or change in quantity demanded will have ramifications for other parts of the value network, resulting in redrawing boundaries between businesses and reforming of clusters. Innovation in any of the five contributors to value can have consequences for the entire value network and can propagate to new markets in each of the element markets.

Summary

A value network consists of the capabilities that culminate in the capacity to deliver products. These capabilities can exist in a number of businesses, which in turn can be members of other clusters and value networks. Three relationships within a value network are identified: a single-sided market relationship in which parties transact directly with one another in a buyer-supplier relationship; a multi-sided market relationship in which parties transact via a platform that is positioned in the value network, between or amongst the participants; and complex relationships due to by-, co- and waste-product considerations that result in dependencies between otherwise separate value networks.

Placing the business in a market provides insight into how the available value added is allocated between the main participants. A broad allocation of value added is determined by the incursion of markets into the value network. The market provides the first cut allocation of value added between parties in the value network. From this starting point the next factors determining the allocation of value added to a party are the value-for-money provided by potential suppliers, the capacity constraints in meeting demand, and strength of the preference to work together in coalitions.

MSPs find a place in the market to facilitate indirect interaction between parties by reducing shared transaction costs. Where positive cross-group effects are generated in the groups of users, the uptake of the platform can be rapid.

Selected literature review

Early origin of idea

The idea that businesses are related by buying inputs and supplying outputs, the basis of a value network, has a long history and was developed by Léon Walras in his writings from 1874. The idea was further developed in the form of input-output tables by Leontief in *Input-Output Economics* published by Oxford University Press in 1966.

The analysis and representation of processes also has a long history, and was systematized by work study pioneer Frank Gilbreth, and presented in the early 1920s.

Key influences on the work

At a practical level, considerations of the production of outputs, using systems and processes from inputs is a central consideration of process engineering. Again this is an area well covered in textbooks on the topic.

The impact of reducing transaction costs and its influence on market structure was a particularly fertile area of strategic management research in the latter half of the twentieth century. One example of this is 'Managing 21st Century Network Organizations' 1992 article by Snow, Miles and Coleman published in *Organisational Dynamics*.

Research into MSPs is a rapidly growing area because of the enormous value that some businesses have been able to achieve. For an introduction to MSPs see the 2011 working paper Hagiu and Wright *Multi-Sided Platforms* from Harvard Business School. The use of participation curves to analyse MSP+s is explored by Evans and Schmalensee in the paper *Failure to launch: Critical mass in platform businesses* published in 2010 in the Review of Network Economics.

For an overview, impact of uncertainty on innovation is reviewed in a 2012 paper by Jalonen 'The uncertainty of innovation: A systematic review of the literature' published in the *Journal of Management Research*.

FOUR
Activity types available to participate in a market

Commonly, a business is thought of as participating in markets by transforming raw materials, using labour and a few tools, into products. This is the simplistic view, portraying production processes used in the arts and crafts. Adam Smith, writing in 1776, attributed the costs of producing products to natural resources including land, human effort and skill from labour, and capital stock such as buildings, machines and tools. Financial capital was not considered a factor of production.

Developing on this thinking in the latter half of the 1800s, Karl Marx determined that the critical factor was labour effort, without which he considered no processes could be performed. Labour effort is applied to natural resources (including land) and raw materials (the subject of labour) using buildings, machines and tools (the means of production). The amount of labour effort is determined by organisation, an element of which is management. Given the social conditions in Industrial Revolution Europe the causal link between labour effort, natural resources, raw materials, means of production and organisation, and profit, may have seemed obvious.

Later economists continued and refined this view of inputs into a production process, but took a wider view on what are called the 'factors of production'. Factors of production now distinguish between financial capital, fixed capital, working capital, and technology. Arguments about the primacy of some factors of production over others have nevertheless continued. In the decades preceding the Global Financial Crisis of 2007 arguments reminiscent of Marx's logic were being used to justify the privileged position that is given to the providers of equity. Indeed this viewpoint is engrained in management studies, with its centre of focus on the 'production function' (whereby, inputs are converted to outputs), and it being distinct from the leadership and other overhead functions. This high level characterisation of the operational activity of business promotes the view that production functions are different because they use different technologies, for example, small-scale batch processes use different technology from large-scale continuous processes.

Introduction

A range of quite different activity types are used to exploit a business opportunity. These activity types give rise to quite different ways to participate in a value network and to share in the available value added. The range is revealed by deriving 16 different activity types. The 16 activity types are applied to a business opportunity to construct 16 different business angles on that opportunity. While these 16 sentinel activity types are used to support the proposition that activity types give rise to different business angles, there are in fact a myriad of different activity types. These, nonetheless, are hybrids of the 16 sentinel activity types. Complex activity type, such as multi-sided platforms, can be analysed using this taxonomy.

This chapter is structured as follows. The next section sets out the taxonomy of 16 sentinel activity types. These activity types are then described in four sections. Hybrid and complex activity types are then discussed.

The range of activity types

Activity types

A production process consists of a set of capabilities to deliver outputs and a set of capabilities to acquire inputs. The framework presented in this section is that specific capabilities are required, first, to produce and deliver each type of product, and second, to acquire and prepare inputs ready for use.

The four generic methods for delivery of outputs are:

- **Assemble method** using knowhow, systems and processes to produce products by exploiting economies of scale and scope. In general, these are products that provide a high degree of readiness for use, through for example, custom, standardisation and specification. This includes consumer products, many of the products that are used to make or provide other products, and raw materials. With these types of products decision-making rights to consume or use are transferred to the buyer on sale, if not entirely, then at least for a period of time.

- **Assign method** producing products that gain efficiencies by improving coordination, by ensuring close alignment of the interests between buyer and supplier. The method provides the capacity to operate a capability enabling businesses to contract-out part of the risk in producing outputs. Outsourcing is an example of products that involve the provision of capacity and the ability to reassign operational risk (and therefore this cost) between parties. The distinguishing feature is the knowhow, systems and processes to operate capabilities to be made available on contract to the buyer.

- **Aggregate method** providing products that depend on the law of large numbers and scale-free infrastructure networks. Examples include creating a portfolio of risky investments with similar characteristics or the aggregation of many small transactions as happens in communications and energy transmission and distribution networks. Insurance is another obvious example. The benefits from risk reassignment are idiosyncratic and provide resilience to businesses to better enable them to cope with specific events that they would otherwise not be able to do.

- **Arbitrage method** involving the knowhow, systems and processes to identify differences in the price of products and assets that are caused by asymmetries in information and high transaction cost. The arbitrage method is the basis of trading and it makes it easier for the buyer to get products. This method relies on transaction specific knowledge, which can arise from barriers to information, location, time, customer relationships, etc.

The four generic methods to acquire and prepare inputs are:

- **Assemble method** involving acquisition of inputs by exploiting economies of scale and scope. These inputs frequently require significant further preparation for use, for example as happens with raw materials. The knowhow, systems and processes may involve logistics, warehousing, inventory management and maintenance of these inputs.

- **Assign method** utilising coordination to ensure close alignment of the interests between buyer and supplier, for example, when contracting for capacity. Commonly this is in the form of outsource relationships or capacity lease contracts. Specific objectives of this type of arrangement are to pass operational risk to the supplier and to reduce the need for capital investment.

- **Aggregate method** involving acquiring inputs to gain the advantages of the law of large numbers and scale-free infrastructure networks. This is achieved by syndicated supply from a large number of similar parties, for instance.

- **Arbitrage method** involving knowhow, systems and processes for the economical purchase of inputs by addressing information asymmetries and high transaction cost.

While not specifically mentioned in the above description, the production processes required by all methods also include appropriate management and financial capabilities to operate a business. There are no overhead capabilities that are separate from a delivery method or an acquisition method. The entire production process used by businesses are specified as delivery and acquisition methods, albeit, some capabilities are used by both delivery and acquisition methods. These capabilities change as the method they are part of change, and do not exist independently of the method.

By characterising the activities of businesses as consisting of delivery and acquisition methods, the four delivery methods and four acquisition methods are combined to give 16 different activity types, and this taxonomy of activity types is set out in Figure 15. Combinations of three or more of these methods are used to generate many more different activity types.

Figure 15 *Taxonomy of activity types*

Method of acquiring inputs	Method of delivering outputs	
	Assemble	*Assign*
Assemble	**a. Producer** Production of products by using inputs that require significant processing. Exploiting declining cost economies that derive from scale and scope to deliver products, and on the inputs used.	**b. Outsource provider** Supply of capacity on the basis of utilising inputs that require significant pre-processing. Exploiting the ability to align the interests between buyer and the provider, and declining cost economies that derive from scale and scope on the inputs used.
Assign	**e. Systems integrator** Production of products utilising contracted operational capacity from third parties. Exploiting declining cost economies that derive from scale and scope to deliver products, and the ability to align the interests between the provider and their suppliers to acquire inputs.	**f. Lead contractor** Supply of capacity by utilising contracted operational capacity from third parties. Exploiting the ability to align the interests between buyers and the provider, and between the provider and their suppliers.
Aggregate	**i. Supplier cooperative** Production of products by engaging with a portfolio of input suppliers. Exploiting declining cost economies that derive from scale and scope to deliver products, and law of large numbers and scale-free infrastructure networks to acquire inputs from suppliers.	**j. Underwriter** Supply of capacity by using capacity syndicated to a number of suppliers. Exploiting the ability to align the interests between buyers and the provider, and law of large numbers and scale-free infrastructure networks to acquire inputs from suppliers.
Arbitrage	**m. Assembler** Production of products on the basis of bought in sub-assembly componentry. Exploiting declining cost economies that derive from scale and scope to deliver products and price differences by utilising asymmetries in access to information, and high transaction costs faced by suppliers.	**n. Broker** Supply of capacity by on-selling capacity from suppliers. Exploiting the ability to align the interests between buyers and the provider, price differences by utilising asymmetries in access to information and high transaction costs faced by the provider and their suppliers.

Method of delivering outputs	
Aggregate	*Arbitrage*
c. Network operator	**d. Developer**
Construction of a portfolio of buyers of products that utilise inputs requiring significant transformation. Exploiting the law of large numbers and scale-free infrastructure networks to deliver products to buyers, and declining cost economies that derive from scale and scope on the inputs used.	Resale of products derived from inputs requiring significant preparation. Exploiting price differences by utilising asymmetries in access to information and high transaction costs faced by buyers, and declining cost economies that derive from scale and scope on the inputs used.
g. Consolidator	**h. Agent**
Construction of a portfolio of buyers of products supplied from operational capacity contracted from third parties. Exploiting the law of large numbers and scale-free infrastructure networks to deliver products to buyers, and the ability to align the interests between the provider and their suppliers.	Resale of contracted operational capacity from third parties. Exploiting price differences by utilising asymmetries in access to information and high transaction costs faced by buyers, and the ability to align the interests between the provider and their suppliers.
k. Insurer	**l. Auctioneer**
Construction of a portfolio of buyers of products that is syndicated to a portfolio of suppliers. Exploiting the law of large numbers and scale-free infrastructure networks to deliver products to buyers and acquire inputs from suppliers.	Resale of products acquired from a range of input suppliers. Exploiting price differences by utilising asymmetries in access to information and high transaction costs faced by buyers, and law of large numbers and scale-free infrastructure networks to acquire inputs from suppliers.
o. Aggregator	**p. Trader**
Construction of a portfolio of buyers for products acquired for reselling. Exploiting the law of large numbers and scale-free infrastructure networks to deliver products to buyers, price differences by utilising asymmetries in access to information and high transaction costs faced by providers and their suppliers.	Trading in products. Exploiting price differences by utilising asymmetries in access to information, and high transaction costs faced by buyers and suppliers.

Different methods exploit different declining cost economies to create core competencies

Declining cost economies are used by businesses to increase value added. These positive feedback economies give a business a cost advantage over its competitors in terms of lower average cost, higher barrier to entry, or lower transaction costs. Declining cost economies are supply-side effects and are different from demand-side effects, such as cross-product and group, and brand loyalty effects, which also create barriers to entry.

The assemble method achieves average cost reduction from declining cost economies that derive from scale and scope. Economies of scale come from falling average costs due to the volume of output. This occurs where high capital investment or high set-up costs (for example, faced by training providers in preparing course content) are involved, and average cost falls with increased output. High volumes of output also provide opportunities for process simplification. Learning from repetition and speed of operation contributes to more efficiency, leading to lower average cost. Other sources of economies of scale are in purchasing, and access to better managerial and technical skills. These latter benefits are also realised from economies of size. Economies of size arise simply because of the size of the business. A large business may, for example, be able to purchase effective advertising more cheaply because of its relatively large spend on advertising. Economies of scope emerge from more product variety. This is most noticeable in better utilising distribution channels, where the addition of similar products reduces the average distribution cost of all products.

The assign method gains efficiencies by improving coordination through ensuring close alignment of the interests between buyer and supplier. There are a number of ways of aligning these interests. These include using incentives and sanctions, close monitoring and formal contracts. Each of these methods imposes costs on the buyer, and are agency costs. Agency costs rise according to the extent of divergence between the interests of the supplier and those of the buyer. Generally speaking, it is more efficient to contract work out than to perform it internally, when: the buyer is able to monitor the performance of external suppliers; the cost of measuring supplier performance will not be out of proportion to the cost of delivering the service; the risk of failure to perform is low, in other words, if an external supplier fails to perform, the ongoing survival of the purchaser will not be threatened; and, large investments in contract specific personnel, systems and processes, and other relationship specific assets are not required. Substantial benefits are gained by the buyer or supplier being able to execute the assign methods well in areas as divergent as building and infrastructure construction and maintenance, through to software development and provision of managed ICT services.

The aggregate method gains cost reductions from the law of large numbers and scale-free infrastructure networks. The law of large numbers applies where, with more occurrences of an unconnected event, the occurrence of an event lies more closely to the average occurrence of the event. To illustrate how economic advantage is gained from this fact, consider a situation where there is a potential loss of $10,000 when an event occurs, and the event occurs on average 1 in 10,000 times in a year, but the number of occurrences that a party faces is unlimited. The loss faced by the party in a year could range from nothing to multiples of $10,000 if they are 'unlucky'. If 10,000 parties were to pool their exposure to the average loss, then the average exposure each party carries is $1 a year. The characteristics of these occurrences are measured and analysed, using statistical techniques to calculate the average and distribution of occurrences. Areas where the law of large numbers applies are: sorts (e.g. mail and parcels), searches (e.g. internet queries), queues (e.g. incoming telephone calls), selection (e.g. purchase of products), data analysis (e.g. weather forecasting), and accidents and errors (e.g. motor vehicle accidents). These events are described by the average and distribution around the average. This is done, for example, by aggregating risks to produce a portfolio with the expected average risk profile. The direct benefit to participants is to spread the cost over all participants. An allied concept is economies from clustering in a geographic location, which due to close proximity, provide cost savings to suppliers or buyers in that location. This has application in distribution networks where, by saturating an area with delivery agents, express point-to-point delivery services can be provided.

Scale-free infrastructure networks derive cost reductions from the design of infrastructure networks, and rely on the role played by hubs with many spokes. In scale-free infrastructure networks hubs with many more than the average number of spokes are comparatively common. A key element of their structure is a hub and spoke, or star network. This network architecture is found in utility, logistic delivery and distributed computing networks. Scale-free infrastructure network architectures exploit the fact that, costs increase linearly with a large number of connections, whereas those for point-to-point networks increase at the square.

The arbitrage method is based on price differences, which arise from barriers caused by asymmetries in access to information and high transaction costs. Information asymmetries apply to all elements that contribute to profit, whether they are internal to the business or stem from market context. The cost advantage this provides arises where it is costly to acquire information, but once gained all subsequent uses of the information are at no additional cost. This means that the average cost of acquiring the information falls exponentially with use. This cost can also arise from uncertainty - for example in a market where some of the items are defective, but this is difficult to assess at the time of purchase. The existence of such 'lemons' reduces the price of good products. The impact of transaction costs is different. The action of these costs is seen in the calculation of the economic order quantity, which is a function of demand, order costs and holding costs. Order costs are those incurred to set up a relationship with a supplier, to place an order, to arrange shipping, shipping and handling on arrival and unpacking. As order costs fall, economic order size falls more rapidly (at the square root).

Different activity types have different characteristics

Different activity types differ in two key characteristics: the operational and financial characteristics. Different activity types are used in a value network to deliver the same end product, but have different ways of achieving this. Using the assign method of acquiring inputs instead of the assemble method can provide a way to make costs variable and reduce capital investment. Contracting for capacity from suppliers is appropriate in rapidly changing markets where demand for a provider's product is uncertain. In contrast, the assemble method requires capital investment, can suffer from capacity constraints, but provides the lowest average cost. Contracting for capacity means that competencies in contracting are developed in the business rather than in processing inputs. Indeed, it is an easily observable fact that different businesses use different combinations of inputs, resources and capital, and earn different rates of returns on investment with different responsibilities for funding losses.

An angle on the business opportunity is the way a business seeks to profit from the opportunity through the use of a particular activity type. The business angle is the selected combination of the value added capture, production process and inputs. Different businesses have different concepts of the way to profit from an opportunity, and indeed different perceptions of the business opportunity, and these are embodied in different product value propositions.

The business angle is demonstrable, described in various business documents such as plans and budgets, and can be communicated to others. The perceived business opportunity, nevertheless, remains a subjective assessment of the opportunity to profit. Products are the contrivance through which market opportunities are pursued and realised. They are needed in order to participate in the cut and thrust of commerce.

Relationship between activity type and operational and financial characteristics

The choice of business angle requires decisions to be made about capital to be invested and risk to be borne. As a general expectation for a specific product, the assemble method involves the greatest level of capital investment and responsibility for carrying the cost of failure. The assign and aggregate methods specifically pass on risk to third parties, and in the case of the assign method this could also involve reduced capital investment. The least capital investment is involved with the arbitrage method. This is a general expectation from the perspective of the entire value network. In the case of businesses delivering products using the assign and aggregate methods, these businesses take on risk from other parties in the value network, and for businesses providing products using the assign method they are also providing capital investment. Businesses engaged in the arbitrage method of providing products also increase the efficiency of the market by facilitating trade in the face of market impediments.

Whilst this is a general expectation, it is not a universal rule on two accounts. Some activity types are infeasible in certain market contexts. The three key variables that determine the range of feasible activity types are the quantity demanded, the rate of market growth, and the rate of change in the market. With high (low) demand, market growth rate, and volatility in the market there will be a high (low) range of feasible activity types. Moreover, substantial businesses are built using each activity type, requiring large capital investment.

The assemble method

Activity types using the assemble method deliver products, and exploit economies of scale and scope in the delivery method. This delivery method, when combined with different acquisition methods, creates different production processes with different characteristics. The different methods of acquiring the inputs employed, are presented in Figure 15:

- *a* — The assemble method uses inputs requiring significant pre-processing.
- *e* — The assign method contracts for operational capacity.

- **i** — The aggregate method engages a portfolio of suppliers to provide inputs.
- **m** — The arbitrage method involves buying sub-assembly componentry.

The assemble method of delivering outputs, when combined with the four methods of acquiring inputs, gives four activity types. On the surface, the four activity types deliver the same output to buyers but differ in: core competencies, and consequently the resources used; how they share in the available value added; and their capital, return and risk profiles. Being different, each of these different production processes is used to create business angles able to cater for different market conditions.

a — The assemble method of delivery with the assemble method of acquisition

Assemble – assemble produces products exploiting declining cost economies that derive from scale and scope to deliver products and to acquire the inputs used. This is the common concept of a business. Businesses using the assemble methods to deliver outputs and acquire inputs create core competencies from scale and scope economies. Essential features of this activity type include being an efficient producer of products from inputs that require significant processing into their output state, and, on sale of products, that transfer the decision-making rights over the use of these products to buyers. Examples of this activity type are found in small family businesses (such as a baker) right through to the largest vertically integrated, multi-divisional multinational corporations. These businesses engage the same activity type using different production technology, and operationally profit is derived from high efficiency in the use of inputs.

e — The assemble method of delivery with the assign method of acquisition

Assemble – assign is based on producing products by utilising declining cost economies that derive from scale and scope to supply products, and the ability to align the interests between the provider and suppliers to acquire inputs. Here production processes are used to coordinate the outsourcing of supply arrangements. Businesses that contract out capabilities or elements of those capabilities apply the assign method to acquire inputs. Core competencies are created from scale and scope economies in the delivery method, and the effective contracting for capacity in the acquisition method by reducing agency costs.

This activity type is widely used by systems integrators, where the relationship with the customer is 'owned' by the business and capability to operate the business's owned plant and equipment is outsourced to a supplier of these capabilities. The unique business objective is the effective and efficient contracting with suppliers of capability. Outsourcing and subcontracting contracts are a means of assigning risk and responsibility for the delivery of certain capabilities to another party for a specified price. The use of this activity incurs transaction costs to contract for, and monitor, supplier performance. However it may not require investment in those capabilities, and passes the operational risk to the supplier.

i — The assemble method of delivery with the aggregate method of acquisition

Assemble – aggregate exploits scale and scope economies in the delivery method, and law of large numbers and scale-free infrastructure networks in the acquisition method to create core competencies to produce products. An illustration of this activity is syndicated supply, for example, with the putting-out system or a farmer-owned cooperative processor. The cooperative invests in the methods for the sale and distribution of products, and end product processing. The production of agricultural produce, an input susceptible to the impact of adverse weather events, is undertaken by a large number of individual farmers who invest in their farming production processes. These individual farmers face strong incentives to achieve higher standards of quality and productivity than could be achieved through other methods of production. For an agricultural cooperative, having a wide geographically dispersed supply base can mitigate the impact of weather on the volume of output, enabling supply contracts to be honoured. For the individual farmer, the cooperative increases average price, the certainty of selling produce, and can provide financial support if any one farmer suffers an adverse event. This activity type, with syndicated inputs, can also be seen in the analysis of data collected from a variety of sources, for example, from logs of retail sales transactions and benchmark surveys, to produce statistical and informational products. Any one of these sources may not be particularly insightful, but combining multiple sources allows computation of useful information.

m — *The assemble method of delivery with the arbitrage method of acquisition*

Assemble – arbitrage uses scale and scope economies in the delivery method, and information asymmetries and transaction costs in the acquisition method. Businesses engaged in this activity produce their own range of products assembled from items produced by others. The items chosen are based on availability and price. Businesses engaged in various assembly operations, such as assembling customised personal computers for on-line gaming, apply this activity.

Core competencies are created from economies in scale and scope in the delivery method, and the asymmetries in access to information and transaction costs are overcome in the acquisition method.

Discussion on the assemble method of delivering products

For a single product using a common delivery method and different acquisition methods, the assemble method of acquisition involves high capital investment. The assign method has lower capital investment because it uses outsourced capacity. The arbitrage method purchases inputs as required. The aggregate method assigns risk to other parties. Using the example of electronics consumer product manufacture, the manufacture of products from component parts is the assemble method, coordinating production using outsourced suppliers is the assign method, and the purchase of standard modules for assembly is the arbitrage method.

Along with the different capital requirement of these four activity types are corresponding differences in the risk profile. The assemble method internalises all operational risks and minimises supplier risk by using standard components. The assign method changes the operational risk by using capability purchased under contract, and this increases supplier risk with the objective of reducing operational risk. The arbitrage method again changes the risk profile, and in particular increases the risk that the bought-in components cannot be successfully integrated, incurring costs to resolve such problems. The aggregate method specifically aims to reduce the cost of risk to the business by placing the supply risk with a number of suppliers.

It is difficult to generalise about how the ability to share in the available value added is changed by the activity type, because this will differ with the particular circumstances facing a business or industry. Nonetheless, it is clear that by changing the capital and risk profile the rate of return on invested capital is changed.

The assign method

This group of activity types delivers products to fulfil a specification or specific mandate by providing capabilities under contract. This differs from the assemble method, which provides outputs where decision-making rights pass on with the product. As an illustration of this difference, a shoe business may design, manufacture and sell shoes and own the manufacturing capability itself. An alternative is for the shoe business to contract out manufacturing to a supplier of shoe manufacturing capacity. The manufacturer providing this capacity may supply it to a number of shoe design and marketing businesses (its customers) with no manufacturing capability.

Activity types using the assign method of delivering outputs (as presented in Figure 15) can acquire inputs by:

- **b** — The assemble method, using inputs requiring significant pre-processing so that the operational risk of doing this is managed in-house.

- **f** — The assign method, in which capacity is acquired from sub-contractors to whom the operational risk is passed, but the business retains the risk of coordinating the various sub-contractors.

- **j** — The aggregate method where capacity requirements are syndicated to a number of suppliers so as to reduce the overall operational risk.

- **n** — The arbitrage method where third parties capacity is on-sold.

b — Assign method of delivery with the assemble method of acquisition

Assign – assemble is an activity that involves supplying capacity on the basis of inputs requiring pre-processing. This activity is usually associated with the provision of outsourced products. It involves businesses that possess superior production processes, and offer products to manage production processes and assets, using their own resources.

This method is based on the provision of capacity to meet a specific requirement. The unique business objective is to provide customers with better value-for-money from buying in capacity, than could be achieved by doing it themselves. This is achieved by operating specialist capacity that sets a higher standard of performance than customers are able to attain themselves. The economics are based on: cost advantages gained from core competencies in providing capacity to buyers with better managed operational risk and lower agency costs; and economies of scale and scope in the acquisition method. The use of contract manufacturing by well-known consumer product brands provides examples of the use of this activity type.

f — Assign method of delivery with the assign method of acquisition

Assign – assign creates clusters of providers of outsource capacity. The value proposition to buyers is that the provider takes on operational risk. The competency of the business is to establish supplier relationships and coordinate the various parties, and in doing so, reduce agency costs in the delivery and acquisition methods.

This activity type is widely used on major construction contracts where various parties come together as a consortium. An illustration of this activity type is public finance initiative special purpose vehicles for infrastructure investment, where the buyer reassigns delivery of products to a head contractor or consortium that, in turn, reassigns components of the project to the members of the consortium – the subcontractors.

j — Assign method of delivery with the aggregate method of acquisition

Assign – aggregate activity reduces agency costs in the delivery method, and the law of large numbers and scale-free infrastructure networks to reduce acquisition costs. This entails a production process to coordinate a large number of parties. The central agent in a putting-out system of work performs this activity. Crowd source platforms for obtaining inputs, such as finance, also perform this activity.

Syndicates, having the competency to identify opportunities that then are able to exploit - by allocating the capacity requirements to a number of suppliers - use this activity type. The economic driver is that by syndicating the capacity requirements to a number of different suppliers the overall risk of failure is reduced, and exposure to loss of any single supplier is reduced to an acceptable level.

n — Assign method of delivery with the arbitrage method of acquisition

Businesses using the **assign – arbitrage** activity supply capacity by creating core competencies, from reduced agency costs in the delivery method, and from reduced costs due to information asymmetries and transaction costs. This is an activity associated with brokers who scout the market for potential opportunities for their client, for a fee, and may then act on behalf of the acquirer to complete the transaction. This activity involves the broker intermediating between buyers (their clients) and sellers, and exploiting their knowledge of both parties' objectives. Brokers are used in a wide range of settings. Examples from the consumer market are real estate and accommodation, mortgage and insurance brokers. In commerce, brokers are active in: purchasing inputs, insurance, finance, and the buying of business assets and equity. Here, the opportunity is associated with exploiting differences in prices.

Discussion on the assign method of delivering products

Businesses that apply the assign delivery method have production processes to provide capacity, and in this way reduce the need for buyers to invest capital, reducing the risk of capacity constraints. A range of sources of declining cost economies are utilised in combination with economies of scale and scope to do this. The capital and risk vary with the acquisition method used. Making sweeping generalisations, the assign delivery method used with the assemble method involves more capital than any of the other acquisition methods. When it is used with the assign and arbitrage acquisition methods, it involves the least. Used with the assign method for acquisition, some intermediate amount of capital is required. The risk profile is quite different with each of the acquisition methods. All operational risk is carried with the assemble method. Agency risk is high with the assign method. The arbitrage method carries high risk that providers may not satisfactorily fulfil contracts. Counterparty risk is a risk that is difficult to assess in advance and is high with the aggregate method.

The aggregate method

A wide range of products are produced in production processes, subject to positive aggregation effects from the law of large numbers and scale-free infrastructure networks. The aggregate method provides buyers access to the benefits of these effects. As presented in Figure 15 this delivery method can be used with the different acquisition methods:

- *c* — To manage the transformation of inputs requiring significant pre-processing, using the assemble method.
- *g* — To acquire operational capacity from third parties, using the assign method.
- *k* — To allocate supply to a syndicate of providers, though the aggregate method.
- *o* — To on-sell inputs, through the arbitrage method.

c — Aggregate method of delivery with the assemble method of acquisition

In **aggregate – assemble,** core competencies are created using the law of large numbers and scale-free infrastructure networks to deliver products utilising economies of scale and scope in the acquisition method. This business angle involves aggregating customers using products that involve, for example, consolidating, queuing, sorting and searching processes. Network operators in communications and distribution frequently fall into this category.

g — Aggregate method of delivery with assign method of acquisition

Aggregate – assign supplies capabilities using portfolio effects from aggregation, using capacity provided on contract. Core competencies are created from the law of large numbers and scale-free infrastructure networks in the delivery method, and the agency costs in the acquisition method. The key distinguishing feature of this activity type, and the one that distinguishes it from the one above, is that parts of the production process are outsourced to other parties. This activity is found in businesses involved in the distribution of energy, phone calls, internet services, letters and parcels.

k — Aggregate method of delivery with aggregate method of acquisition

The heart of the **aggregate – aggregate** activity is exploiting the law of large numbers and scale-free infrastructure networks for both the delivery of products and the acquisition of inputs to create core competencies. Businesses involved in book-building and repackaging of assets, to change their financial profile, use this activity type. This is undertaken with insurance and debt instruments.

For example, a portfolio of insurance policies over residential properties can be created for a particular locality, and this will have high exposure to risks, such as earthquakes, peculiar to that geographic location. Through reinsurance the geographic risk can be combined with other geographic locations thereby reducing the insurer's exposure of loss from that particular event. Introduction services also use this activity. Introduction services operate in a range of settings, from arranging personal introductions to introducing would-be investors to businesspeople.

o — *Aggregate method of delivery with arbitrage method of acquisition*

The **aggregate – arbitrage** activity exploits the law of large numbers and scale-free infrastructure networks in the delivery method, and information asymmetries and high transaction costs in the acquisition method. This activity type is found in collective buying, insurance and investment schemes. A buyer cooperative aggregates purchase orders from its members before tendering these to potential suppliers.

Discussion on the aggregate method of delivering products

Businesses accessing declining cost economies from law of large numbers and scale-free infrastructure networks in the delivery method are found using all the available methods of acquisition. At a high level of generalisation, the assemble method involves more capital than the arbitrage method, and the assign and aggregate methods involve a medium amount. This generalisation should not be taken to imply that methods other than the assemble method do not involve very substantial capital bases, or involve very high levels of risk. Businesses using these activity types can create very valuable scarce resources.

The arbitrage method

Many highly profitable businesses are founded on developing the ability to identify and deliver on business opportunities that utilise information asymmetries and high transaction costs. Illustrations of this type of business are found in design and asset development, agents, auction houses and trade. The competency of operators providing services based on this method is in, first, recognising the opportunity, which can be a one-off situation; second, being able to earn a profit from it; and third, being able to use this capability on a continuous basis. The four activity types (as presented in Figure 15) use the arbitrage delivery method in conjunction with:

- **d** — The assemble method, involving inputs requiring significant pre-processing. An example is property developers with construction capabilities, who identify sites for development or redevelopment, then gain development rights for that site, and then sell the redevelopment to prospective buyers - frequently from the plans.

- **h** — The assign method, utilising operational capacity from third parties. An example is agents who act for other parties under contract. This includes manufacturer representatives who are able to locate buyers on behalf of the seller. These agents act under contract to the seller and do not gain ownership of the product.

- **l** — The aggregate method, in which inputs are acquired from a range of suppliers. An example is auction houses/websites, and commodity exchanges that operate in a range of setting from second-hand items to fine art and precious metals and other commodities.

- **p** — The arbitrage method, in which inputs are acquired for resale – this is the trader who finds opportunities with a buyer and/or seller, and a way of fulfilling the trade.

d — *The arbitrage method of delivery with the assemble method of acquisition*

Arbitrage – *assemble* activity exploits price differences using a business's own resources. Price differences arise from information asymmetries and high transaction costs and, combining this with acquisition methods, the business is able to gain economies of scale and scope. This is a well-known activity in real estate property development, but has its parallel more generally in businesses that redevelop assets from a lower price use into an alternative higher price use. The economics are based on asymmetries, which derive from delivering products to customers that are more costly to do on their own. This activity type requires continuous effort to balance the hunt to find new work, while maintaining the right mix of resources to be able to take on the risk of delivering the expected quality, in time and within budget. Businesses operating in this area have the ability to scan the market for opportunities, and the knowhow, systems and processes to deliver on the opportunity using in-house resources. Professional services such as merchant banks and management consultancies operate this activity type.

h — *The arbitrage method of delivery with the assign method of acquisition*

The **arbitrage – *assign*** activity exploits price differences using capabilities from contracted suppliers of capacity. Core competencies are created from taking advantage of asymmetries in information and reducing transaction costs in the delivery method, and reducing agency costs in the acquisition method. This activity type involves seeking out opportunities, and then finding ways to facilitate meeting that need from existing capacity available in the market. Examples of this activity are capacity brokers who sell, for example, surplus warehouse capacity, and executive lease agencies who market the skills of the experienced personnel they have on their books. Businesses that facilitate capacity sharing in minicabs and holiday homes also use this activity type.

l — *The arbitrage method of delivery with the aggregate method of acquisition*

Arbitrage – *aggregate* exploits price differences in the delivery method, combined with the law of large numbers and scale-free infrastructure networks in the acquisition method. Auction houses/websites utilise this activity type by providing a place for a large number of sellers to have their products sold, on the basis of the price offered by buyers. Another example of this activity type is agricultural commodity exchanges, where many small producers of coffee or cocoa beans are able to sell their produce to large buyers. Without the exchange, the cost of dealing with small producers is too high and large buyers may then prefer to deal only with large suppliers.

This activity type is also associated with special purpose syndicated financing. It involves a business having the competency to identify opportunities that are able to exploit differences in businesses evaluation of risk, or the law of large numbers in altering risk profiles. The business model involves repackaging risk whilst minimising the business's own exposure to loss in performing this activity. Businesses operating this activity type have comparatively low capital requirements, but can face substantial loss due to poor management of the exposure to risk.

p — The arbitrage method of delivery with the arbitrage method of acquisition

Arbitrage – arbitrage exploits price differences in both input and output markets. The activity type can entail exploiting information asymmetries and high transaction costs by buying assets for resale at a higher price. A wide range of commerce is involved with exploiting this activity type, and is most commonly associated with the retail and wholesale trade. At the simplest it involves correcting observed differences in prices. The business model is to win sales on the basis of knowing what deals are to be done in the market. Transactions of this type can involve high exposure to losses by making decisions that turn out to be wrong. As a simple example, a retailer anticipating a wet winter may buy in a stock of raincoats. If the winter turns out to be dry, the retailer is left at the end of the season with stock of unsold raincoats which have then to be sold at a discount.

Discussion on the arbitrage method of delivering products

The first observation about the arbitrage method of delivering products and the allocation of capital and risk, is that in comparison to the other acquisition methods, the arbitrage method is inherently the most risky. It is also, in a comparative sense for a common product, the least capital intensive. Nonetheless, activity types using the arbitrage method of delivering products can involve very substantial sums of money.

Hybrids and complex activity types

Hybrid activity types

Hybrids of activity types utilise more than two sources of declining cost economies in the delivery and acquisition methods to form an activity type. Businesses use whatever mix of declining cost economies they are able to, not limiting their choice to the 16 sentinel activity types. It is possible to design production processes combining the sources of declining economies in different combinations to create hybrid activity types. As one simple example, department stores use a delivery method combining the aggregate and arbitrage methods.

Complex activity types

Businesses create complex activity types by operating more than one method of delivering outputs and acquiring inputs, alongside one another. To illustrate this, consider a value network centred on a business with established marketing and distribution capabilities. The product it sells could be acquired by adopting three methods: using in-house capacity; outsourcing to tied suppliers for contracted capacity; or purchasing capacity from independent suppliers to cope with peak requirements. The use of tied suppliers gives the business certainty of supply for worst case, lowest demand conditions, while also providing flexibility to acquire additional product where market demand warrants it. From this arrangement the tied supplier has the certainty of always selling their output at an agreed proportion of the final sale price. If all methods of supply face the same production cost, then if tied suppliers are paid a fixed percentage of the final sale price for the product, they will supply a lesser quantity than would be produced in-house. This is appropriate where the business prefers to enter into a long-term commitment for secure supply, as additional volume could be purchased from independent suppliers should demand exceed this level. By using several acquisition methods, a business has a way of dealing with uncertainty in demand.

Application to exploiting cross-group effects

Examples of complex activity types are those used by MSP+s, which are derived from cross-group effects where each side of the platform is supported by a delivery method. MSP+s use a hybrid activity type. The aggregate method is used predominantly to deliver products to the two groups of users, with secondary use of the assign method. Most inputs are acquired by simple contracts (assemble method), with some contracting out (assign method).

Summary

The wide range of quite different activity types provides many ways to pursue a perceived business opportunity. Activity types use different sources of declining cost economies to create value. Declining cost economies include those associated with: scale and scope; the law of large numbers and scale-free infrastructure networks; agency costs, and information asymmetries and high transaction costs. The coupling of the opportunity and activity types is the business angle through which the perceived opportunity is to be exploited. A taxonomy of 16 sentinel activity types is outlined, based on the use of four methods of delivering outputs and four methods of acquiring inputs. Examples of the sentinel activity types are:

a. **Producer:** assemble – assemble activity type.

b. **Outsource provider:** assign – assemble activity type.

c. **Network operator:** aggregate – assemble activity type.

d. **Developer:** arbitrage – assemble activity type.

e. **Systems integrator:** assemble – assign activity type.

f. **Lead contractor:** assign – assign activity type.

g. **Consolidator:** aggregate – assign activity type.

h. **Agent:** arbitrage – assign activity type.

i. **Supplier cooperative:** assemble – aggregate activity type.

j. **Underwriter:** assign – aggregate activity type.

k. **Insurer:** aggregate – aggregate activity type.

l. **Auctioneer:** arbitrage – aggregate activity type.

m. **Assembler:** assemble – arbitrage activity type.

n. **Broker:** assign – arbitrage activity type.

o. **Aggregator:** aggregate – arbitrage activity type.

p. **Trader:** arbitrage – arbitrage activity type.

Activity types also differ in:

- The core competencies used.
- The product benefit attributes offered.
- The place in the value network.

- Ways to allocate capital and risk.
- The ability to deal with market instability (inhibited by management structures and objectives).
- The ability to capture value.

Hybrid activity types are created from these 16 sentinel activity types by combining several methods of delivery outputs with several methods of acquiring inputs. Businesses create complex activity types by operating more than one method of delivery outputs and acquiring inputs alongside one another.

Selected literature review

Early origin of idea

Interest in the systematic design of production processes goes back to the mid Nineteenth Century as illustrated by Charles Babbage's 1832 publication *On the Economy of Machinery and Manufactures*.

Key influences on the work

Analysis of the systematic classification of production technologies to enable the choice of an appropriate process emerged in the late 1970s, see for instance Terry Hill's book *Production/Operations Management* published by Prentice/ Hall International in 1983. This is a topic now covered in texts on process and industrial engineering.

FIVE

The market for financial assets provides ways to share in a business opportunity

In the mid-1860s the West Coast Gold Rush was underway in New Zealand, attracting a large influx of miners from around the world to work the alluvial deposits with tools that required little capital investment. These deposits were soon exhausted and interest shifted to mining the gold bearing quartz seams in the hills surrounding Reefton, in particular.

Quartz mining, and extraction of the metal, is in comparison capital intensive, requiring investment in labour and machinery to develop access to the site, shaft mining, rock crushing and gold extracting. Capital was raised for many of these ventures by issuing share certificates. There was a ready supply of shares. Over 60 quartz mining companies had been floated by the end of 1871. This capital was drawn from locals who included the miners, their employers, local business proprietors, as well as others such as farm workers and people living outside the district. These were highly speculative ventures, with a few spectacular successes paying large dividends, but most of these mines failed. The price of shares fluctuated widely, and at the peak of the activity share prices were published twice daily.

Operating in this market were people who helped put together prospectuses to be distributed to potential investors in new mines, brokers who traded shares, and a stock exchange from which brokers operated and settlement took place. This phase of speculative mining in the Reefton area came to a crashing halt in 1883, with investors losing confidence. Share prices plummeted and investors were not prepared to invest to develop mines. Most of these mining ventures were forced to close.

The next phase of gold mining speculation in Reefton, requiring much higher levels of capital investment to work deeper deposits, commenced in the late 1890s. For this phase capital was raised through the London Stock Exchange. In a matter of thirty or so years, investment had shifted from being sourced from the participants themselves, to the local community, through to international investors.

Introduction

The FCF value of a business is increased by making improvements to any, or all, of the key contributors to value, which are: revenues from value-for-money products; selection of inputs for a highly productive production process and economical purchasing of inputs; high productivity and effective production process; valuable scarce resources underpinned by appropriate risk mitigants, strategic options and financial management of the business. Each of these contributors operates in a market, and the expectation is that improved performance in any of these contributors, above that achieved by competitors, will improve the value of the business. In addition, businesses are able to increase value by increasing the market value of assets, and the business itself. The value of assets is influenced by their characteristics, liquidity, how they are packaged and marketed, market demand and financial use - be it for the sale of assets and equity, or as security for debt finance. As with the first law of thermodynamics, where heat flows from a warmer to a colder body, capital flows from low to high expected return uses and, in addition, the rate of that flow increases as the expectation of future capital flows. Where there is an opportunity for such a flow there is a business opportunity to try to share in the flow.

Compared to other markets, financial markets are liquid, vast and sophisticated; consisting of a range of different value networks that intersect with all other value networks. Financial markets are pervasive. The value created in non-financial markets is realised in financial markets through access to capital and financial transactions. The supply and demand dynamics of financial markets can at times appear to be unrelated to those of the underlying business and its assets, and this creates additional business opportunities to capture part of the money flow. These flows can be substantial.

This chapter discusses how activity types are used to create financial assets with desired capital, risk and return profiles to exploit different orders of market play. Five orders of market play are available to share in the value from a value network. Designing activity type to cater for market and businesspeople's conditions lowers the barriers to entry and increases the supply of capital to exploit a perceived opportunity. This can affect the price of assets and equity, and can substantially change the flow of money, opening up opportunities for speculation. This is explored in the following section. Discussion then focuses on the five orders of market play, and the activity types that are used to participate in these financial flows.

Financial assets as products

Financial assets created from cash flows

There are a plethora of financial products, including assets, splits and leverages, and portfolios. Identifying financial assets involves being able to specify assets that can be priced by the market. This might involve a change in use and packaging to make it sellable, such as listing ownership interests on an exchange. Strips are elements of cash flow that can be specified as a flow of benefits from a resource, or cash flow commitment with specific attributes. Allied to this is the ability to use these attributes to gain better terms and conditions on contracts, for example, by leveraging assets. Portfolios or books are aggregations of financial assets whose capital, risk and return profile derives from its average performance.

Financial products are used in a wide range of settings. A few well established illustrations are: sharing in the ownership of assets; providing capital to new or high risk ventures; enabling access to resources on agreed payment terms with tax advantages (leasing arrangements are an example of this); and improving liquidity (for example, by providing accounts receivable factoring). There is wide familiarity that rights to ownership or control of assets have market value, which can be realised through sale. Financial markets price a wide variety of assets. As with other products, weak demand for an asset is reflected in lower price. In some cases, for instance, for assets where there is a limited market, special techniques have been developed to estimate value to facilitate their sale. Many financial transactions are based on estimates of the market value of assets. Valuations form the basis of a wide variety of financial transactions, including access to bank loans. For businesses, there are two significant factors in assessing value, first is liquidity in the form of expected cash flow over the period under consideration, and second, the market value on the business (which could be the liquidation value of the assets it owns or controls). A wide variety of methods are used to estimate liquidity and value, and some by convention are used in specific industries. A multiple of earnings in the recent past is commonly used to value an established small business as a going concern in mature industries. For new businesses, especially those based on technology that are highly scalable with potential for rapid growth, cash flow budgets are used to establish a 'cash burn rate' until the venture turns cash flow positive, and the FCF value is widely used as a basis for business valuation. This definition of an asset is different from that used in financial accounting, as its focus is entirely on expected market value, either for individual assets, or the business as a whole, whereas financial accounting gives recognition to past transactions.

Despite the difficulties caused by uncertainty, anything that is priced can be arbitraged. Subject to legal constraints, almost any asset, including expected future cash flows, are traded or hold potential to be traded. As a traded asset, they are subject to the forces of supply and demand. Financial assets are also 'manufactured' to meet a perceived demand at a profit. Not only does the manufacture of financial assets represent an extensive range of business opportunities, but the crafting of the value of a business to improve its market value is an element in the design of a business angle.

Financial assets created using contractual commitments

'Contractual commitments' arise from express terms and conditions between the parties to an agreement, sometimes in the form of a legally binding agreement. Contractual commitments are intertwined with the business's dealings in all element markets. Importantly contractual claims can create assets as well as liabilities for the business. These contracts are bilateral or trilateral. GAAP and tax authorities have specific rules for the treatment of some contractual commitments.

A range of business opportunities are associated with changing the terms and conditions of the ownership or control of assets. These can include using contractual commitments to create financial products out of resources, asset repackaging, and risk and income allocation. For example, a resource is a source or supply of profit. To illustrate this, real estate property is easily recognised as an asset, while the flow of benefits it provides (such as shelter, prestige) is a resource. By creating a lease the real estate is split into two contractual components, the resource (the leasehold) and ownership of the freehold title to a leasehold property. Many potential assets are unpriced, as a business has either no plans for selling them, or has no independent basis on which to estimate market value.

Alternative funding arrangements are used when the business has mostly unpriced assets such as software under development, and is engaged in R&D where new knowledge is being developed, because asset value is much less than the FCF value. Contractual commitments enable the mixing of equity and debt funding – more debt funding tends to be used where asset value is high, and more equity funding used where the business has more unpriced assets. In R&D based businesses there is a strong relationship between the creation of valuable core competencies based on past success. This is used to access equity funding to finance R&D rich business angles.

Manufacture of financial products

The ability to create financial products is a central consideration in selecting some business angles. This is because activity type is a determinant of capital, risk and return characteristics, and can be used to craft a desirable net cash flow profile. Other considerations in designing high market value financial products are: the selection of type of financial product for which high demand exists; and the form of the financial product to enable efficient buying and selling of the asset. This might be done, for example, in a setting where there is an asset bubble for investment in a certain class of asset. These bubbles occur from time-to-time in markets for fine and contemporary art, technology start-up businesses, production of agriculture products and real estate, for example. Suppose the value of a vineyard business is attributed to two key drivers: FCF value and timing of cash flow. The choice of activity type on these variables is used to create different financial assets with different capital, risk and return profiles. New businesses can be created using the *assemble-assign* activity type with investment made only in land and buildings, and supply contracts for land development, viticulture, wine making and marketing. This business could be generating an income several years after establishment. The rapid growth following start-up possible by using the *assign-assign* activity type can be used to create an "aggressive growth" financial asset, whereas the slower growth in value using the *assemble-assemble* activity type creates a more moderate growth financial asset.

The creation of financial assets in each of the element markets

As financial assets are assets (capital assets) their value is derived from contractual claims and they can be created in each of the element markets in which a business operates. Stocks and shares are a well-known type of financial asset created from ownership interests in businesses. Debt securities (such as bonds and debentures) and derivatives (such as future contracts) are applied in product and commodity markets. Financial assets have attributes of value, uncertainty and cash flow, derived from some specified source. These attributes are combined to create new hybrid products.

Financial assets have a number of features. They can be more liquid than the underlying tangible assets, such as real estate, and in some cases are traded on financial markets. For some financial assets, there is legislation in some jurisdictions governing their issue and use.

Financial assets and scarce resources

The return on scarce resources is the outturn from the actual use of resources to capture, for the business, a share of the available sales. The business plan sets out: how scarce resources are to be created, enhanced and used operationally; the competitive actions to be taken; and the timing and nature of strategic decisions to be made. While still in the planning stage, strategic options remain open, and the implied cost of holding them open is the option premium. As the business plan is executed, options are exercised or abandoned and the option premium changes.

The option premium gives recognition to the portfolio of salient strategic options and constraints that the business faces in participating in a market. Even where these are not explicitly managed, businesses are continually changing the composition of their portfolio of options. This occurs in parallel with changes in the mix of constraints that are faced. Some of these options and constraints remain relevant and roll over from one period to the next. Some new options and constraints will be acquired or incurred. Some options will be executed or allowed to expire, and some constraints will be reduced or removed. This process of managing a portfolio of options and constraints is one of the key roles of management. While the maintenance of options comes at a cost, the payback is from the increase in FCF value.

Businesspeople are in the business of creating, acquiring, managing and selling scarce resources in their pursuit of exploiting perceived business opportunities. There are two related facets to this. The first is generating profits from accessible markets using available resources. Second, pursuit of profit focuses on the ability of businesses to generate value into the future. This means in addition to the drive to improve performances in respect of revenues, operating costs, risk allocation and asset utilisation, there are significant opportunities to grow the profit through growth in market value of scarce resources and the business as a going concern. In short, one aim of business endeavour is to realise value through the sale of scarce resources, and all or part of the ownership rights to the business itself.

Increasing value from declining cost economies, ability to realise plans, and capacity to respond

The counterfactual to the current use of resources is the return from any alternative use of those resources. Other alternatives available are to sell the business as a going concern, or to wind the business up and sell its assets. These alternatives are selected where the value from any of these alternatives exceeds the FCF value from continuing to operate and/or own the current business. The difference between current use of resources or ownership, and the alternative, is the opportunity cost. The opportunity cost is the net benefit forgone by pursuing the best alternative course of action. Despite being called the opportunity cost, the net benefit forgone can be positive or negative. A business with valuable scarce resources derived from declining cost economies, and ability to realise plans and a portfolio of options to provide flexibility, could face a net cost if it were to deploy its resources in any other use. Similarly, a potential buyer could assess the value of a business as higher than the seller's plans, where the buyer, by combining with their existing resources, is able to improve the overall FCF value from improvements in declining cost economies, and has the ability to realise plans and portfolio of options to provide resilience against the impact of uncertainty.

Price speculation

The value attributed to a business's plans is its FCF value. Any difference between the FCF value of the business and what others will pay for it (the market value) is a potential source of speculative gains. Opportunities for different assessments of the value of a business multiply when there is a range of different viewpoints on the profits that it can achieve; for example, by changing the use of assets. The extent of speculation is often assessed as the difference between the market value of assets (including shares, commodities, land and buildings) and their FCF value. A result is that an opportunity for speculative profit occurs where the market price has the potential to be greater than the current income earning ability of resources in their current planned use.

Figure 16 illustrates the deviation of market prices for a scarce resource from the expected price. The left hand graph shows the market price of a scarce resource compared to its expected price at three successive points in time (T_1, T_2, and T_3). Where market value is above expected price, more of the resource will be created, and supply of new scarce resources will continue for as long as market price is above the expected value. An asset price bubble exists for as long as market price is above expected value. The lifecycle of the bubble is shown in the right hand graph. The left hand graph also shows how, in a speculative bubble, the demand curve can shift to the right as more people become interested in speculating on the asset.

Figure 16 *Illustration of the deviation of market prices for a resource from the expected price using demand a supply curves at three points in time (T1, T2 and T3)*

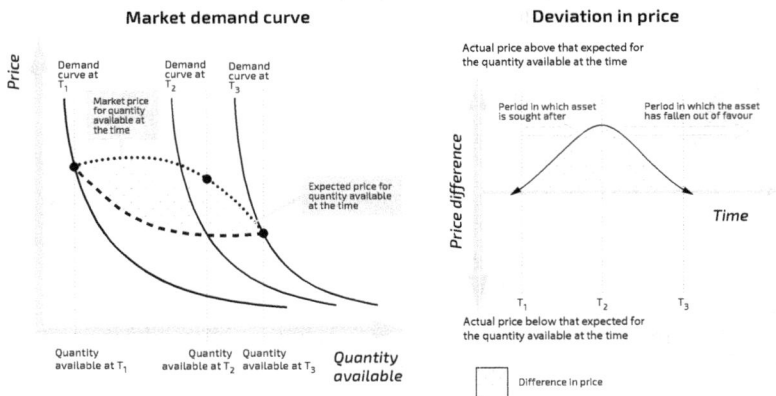

Speculation leading to significant deviation of market value from FCF value is attributed to the way investors behave in markets, and their expectations of the future. A wide variety of explanations have been put forward to account for these behavioural aspects of business decisions, for example intragroup effects such as the bandwagon effect and zeitgeist. Asset price bubbles can occur and persist even when most investors know that the price is too high. These may persist because of differences of opinion about when the trend will reverse. If some investors believe that the market has not peaked (bottomed) and will continue to climb (fall), they may choose to continue investing (divesting). Reinforcing this, any ambiguity in market data is a source of uncertainty in decisions. Ambiguity arises where the information available is not specific enough, or can be misinterpreted, or where more than one explanation is possible. The overall implication is that the FCF value for a business will deviate from its market value in some unknown and unknowable way.

Returning to the example of real estate investment, if the market value of the real estate rental business were more than the market value of the assets plus the FCF value, then the higher value ascribed by the market to the business is a speculative gain. The owner of the business could realise the speculative gain by selling it for market value. This ability of assets to have different values to different businesspeople is an important source of both business innovation and market dynamism.

Actual profit varies from expected profit because of deviations from planned revenues and cost. These variations are attributed to uncertainty in actual performance. Uncertainty is a ubiquitous cost to business, and it impacts on profitability. Like many other aspects of commerce, the size of this cost is unknown in advance (even though its key drivers can be identified). A manifestation of uncertainty is volatility in asset prices. Uncertainty makes predicting future FCF value more difficult, and prices more turbulent. Faced with uncertainty, buyers are less willing to take a positive position for a specific asset. This is a cost to business.

The option premium reflects the cost of holding open choices that will enable the business to respond to circumstances, and either maintain or enhance their future income earning ability. In contrast, the uncertainty premium is concerned with ensuring that there are appropriate resources to enable the business plan to be realised.

Strategic options and uncertainty mitigation mechanisms have different roles to perform. Because both require the commitment of resources, decisions made in respect of either one can impact on the other. To minimise capital requirements a business may choose to outsource some systems and processes. With an appropriate contract, this may also provide the business with the ability to scale the capacity required. On the other hand, outsourcing this capability means that the business is not building up core competencies in that area. Were that capability to emerge as a scarce resource, the outsourced supplier may capture a disproportionate share of the value added. Although the option and uncertainty premiums are different in the purposes they serve, decisions made to manage each can impact the other.

Orders of market play

The demand for, and supply of, financial products are used to exploit business opportunities in five orders of market play. While other products also use these orders of market play, financial products provide examples to explain the orders that involve making products by:

- Working within a value network *(Order 1)*.
- Aiming to reform a value chain and its markets *(Order 2)*.
- Changing the flow of money between the different participants and markets in different value networks *(Order 3)*.

- Fuelling fads and bubbles **(Order 4)**.
- Exploiting performance ambiguity **(Order 5)**.

Order 1 — Working within the value network

Businesses are involved in the market to the first order, where they produce financial products within a definable value network, in the sense that they are able to lay claim to a share of the available value added in that value network. Businesses engaged in the production of products in a market with known conditions, are involved in the market to the first order, if this is all they do, to lay claim to a share of the available value added in the value network by working with the known unknowns. The vast majority of business activity operates in Order 1 – seeking to share in the available value added in a value network.

Order 2 — Market disruption

Businesses that actively seek to disrupt existing markets, to increase their share of available value added, participate in the market to the second order as they seek to change the shape of the value network. For the second order of market play businesses are engaged in transforming a value network. Businesses engage in disrupting a market in a number of ways, including pricing, product innovation, transforming the meaning of the product to increase the value-for-money, and changing the number of stages in a value network with the aim of exploiting differences in the nature of the demand relationship between each successive stages in the value network. The latter could be in the form of arbitraging or the creation of a multi-sided market. Some businesspeople actively seek to provide finance to ventures that hold the prospect of disrupting a market.

Order 3 — Changing the flow of money

Change in asset value impacts on the flow of money. Businesses that aim to re-price assets with the objective of changing the weight of the flow of money, so as to capture a part of those flows, participate in the market to the third order. The business opportunity is to 'clip the ticket' on these money flows.

Order 4 — Fuelling fads and bubbles

The fourth order involves exploiting asset bubbles and fads. These businesses rely on rapid changes in asset values and having the competencies to exploit this type of opportunity. While some bubbles can last many years, many are short-lived. Consequently, businesses operating at this order of market play are always on the lookout for the next 'big thing'. Brokers, promoters and developers of products to satisfy the demand for this type of asset fall into this category.

Order 5 — Exploiting performance ambiguity

Businesses producing products whose quality or efficacy is difficult to establish, and using these conditions to encourage the mispricing or the misplacement of trust, are engaged in the fifth order of market play. Examples of this type of business opportunity are far-ranging and include participation in creating sham assets during an asset bubble, celebrity endorsement of products with little appreciation of the characteristics of the product being endorsed, alternative health products with unsubstantiated health benefits, premiums extracted from the sale of hyped up shares in 'goldilocks' businesses, and on through to Ponzi schemes promising unbelievably good returns to investors. At their heart, these market offerings exploit asymmetries in knowledge (sometimes created fraudulently) and performance ambiguity in assessing short-term performance. These opportunities also include products to address information asymmetries to mitigate the cost of misplaced trust, such as financial auditing, probity reviews, credit ratings, and independent quality assessments of large complex projects.

Participation in multiple orders of market play

While an opportunity may on the surface be easy to categorise, by their nature higher orders of market play can be hidden or disguised as lower order market plays, and this may not become clear until much later – frequently when significant losses are experienced in that higher order of market play. A business can be predominantly engaged in one order of market play and only occasionally venture into others, although most are not engaged in the fifth order of market play. Nor, it should be added, are all businesses inclined to be involved in multiple orders of market play. Each order of market play involves investment in knowhow, systems and processes to give effect to a business angle. Different orders of market play involve exploiting a suite of different business angles with underpinning activity types.

An illustration drawn from the banking and finance industry in the lead up to the Global Financial Crisis of 2007 is that some of the financial instruments created purposefully set out to manipulate markets, and did so, so profoundly that they reshaped value networks. At the time it might have been seen that these businesses were competing to change capital flows in their favour, a third order play. In hindsight it is now clear that these businesses created financial products that in effect placed risk with tax payers, and for this reason they were engaged in fifth order market play.

Sources of business opportunities

The demand for, and supply of, financial products creates two sources of business opportunities; one is the business angles that give rise to financial assets, and the other is the business angles that are involved in the manufacture and trade of financial products.

Business angles that give rise to financial assets

As discussed earlier, businesspeople can improve a business's value by developing valuable core competencies, assets that are worth more to others, and equity attractive to investors. Starting with a clean sheet, the capital, risk and return characteristics of a business are crafted to create financial securities for sale, to meet a perceived demand, at a profit. The choice of business angle changes the capital, risk and return profile of a business. This is demonstrated by the fact that each of the 16 sentinel activity types could be utilised to create financial assets with different characteristics. Less freedom is available when securities are created for the sale of an existing business or where the business angle has already been chosen. Nonetheless, there is a wide range of ways that existing assets can be leveraged into new opportunities.

A value controller in a value network is a business with high bargaining power that exerts a high degree of control over the allocation of value added in a value network, and has the ability to dictate, at least for a period of time, the pace of change in the value network. The degree to which the value controller is able to maintain this position will depend on how well they are able to maintain alignment between the first three orders of market play. These give market power. To be in control of a value network requires leadership in each order. The ability of a participant in a value network to become a value controller changes the flow of money in the value network, and this in turn can alter the uncertainty faced by the value network. A consequence of this could be to create new opportunities in each of the orders of market play.

Business angles that are involved in the manufacture and trade of financial products

As with any other perceived business opportunity, businesspeople go about exploiting opportunities in the manufacture and trade of financial products, in any of the five orders of market play, using different activity types to craft a business angle with the desired capital, risk and return profile.

Business opportunities associated with each order of market play

Orders of market play in the element markets

While these five orders of market play are introduced using financial market examples they also apply in non-financial markets. Even when applied in non-financial markets the benefits are frequently reaped through financial markets by use of contractual commitments. For business planning and budgeting purposes the interactions that take place in each market are usually analysed separately.

Each of the 16 sentinel activity types could be utilised to exploit perceived opportunities in each of the five orders of market play. This does not mean that, at any point in time, all 16 sentinel activity types are either feasible or viable, as that depends on the particular characteristics in the market at the time. Each activity type creates different products, the structure of value networks and financial assets (with different capital, risk and return characteristics). Financial assets with different characteristics are generated at each order of market play. This ability to generate financial assets with different characteristics, through choice of level of market play and business angle, is used to manufacture financial assets with characteristics that are in demand in the market. In this way, higher orders of market play not only create opportunities for new investment but create avenues for on-going investment through financing disruptive market plays.

An example of different orders of market play is found in consumer payment products. Payments can be made using cash and cheque provided by retail banks - this was Order 1.

Credit cards disrupted this form of payment by providing a consumer finance and transaction mechanism, with lower transaction costs, that was a better value proposition to both merchants and shoppers. The investment to establish credit card businesses was an Order 2 type market play. Credit cards were in turn challenged and their value proposition undermined by direct debit cards and internet banking. The founders of the major credit card businesses realised the value of their investment by selling the businesses through public share offerings – an Order 3 market play. The sale of these businesses would be Order 4, if businesses had been manufactured explicitly for sale at the time of an equity bubble. It would be an Order 5 market play had it emerged that the businesses had misrepresented the quality of their consumer loan portfolio by lending to people unable to repay the debt.

The economic impact of speculation

The fact that a business angle type can be designed to cater for buyer demand, and the businessperson's circumstances, lowers the barriers to entry to exploit a perceived opportunity and, consequently, increases the supply of investment because capital, risk and return profiles can be engineered to meet buyer's requirements. The higher orders of market play do not just capture value added from lower orders of market play, they in their turn can add value by removing inefficiency and stimulating innovation. This is achieved by increasing the forecast income from speculation, reducing the expected uncertainty and option premiums. For this reason, far from being a 'parasite' preying on lower orders of market play, higher orders increase the vigour of the economy.

The beauty of markets is that they are quite unlike this prey-predator model, in that the opportunity to speculate, when there is a perceived regularity in the data, can fuel speculative bubbles. Speculative bubbles are associated with substantial flows of money. These flows can cause distortions to the rest of the economy where they involve assets required to meet basic needs, such as residential housing, energy and food.

Summary

Businesses create assets. Activity types enable a range of financial assets with different value, cash flow and uncertainty characteristics that can be developed to pursue a perceived business opportunity. These ways, in turn, represent further sources of business opportunities.

Assets have at least two values, one attributed to the net cash flow and its timing when compared to the discount rate, which is referred to as the FCF value. The other value is a market price. The market price is usually different from the FCF value. There are a number of reasons why this could be so, one being its liquidity. Poor liquidity can severely impede the market value of an asset, in some cases making it worthless. Market value can differ from FCF value for sustained periods of time. An asset bubble exists when the market value is above the FCF value for a sustained period of time. The deviation of market value from FCF value creates an opportunity for profit from speculation.

Business angles seek to extract value from a value network. Financial asset markets facilitate the use of different orders of market play. The first order involves laying claim to a share of the available value added in the value network. The second order covers opportunities from changing the value network. The third order entails gaining a share of the flow of money from re-pricing assets.

The fourth order opportunities are associated with fads and bubbles. The fifth order accounts for the actions of those who exploit situations where trustworthiness cannot be easily established.

Selected literature review

Early origin of idea

Financial capital as a tool of entrepreneurship has a long history. To account for this use of capital, merchants and bankers in medieval Venice, Florence and Genoa developed the double entry bookkeeping system. Central to this system is the identity *Owners Equity = Assets – Liabilities.* These Medieval merchants and bankers clearly knew that the supply of capital provides ways to share in business opportunities. Their success financed the Renaissance.

Key influences on the work

Discussion and the explanation for financial products is the topic of the many textbooks on corporate finance.

SIX

The opportunity focused business parlays its position into new business angles

In the late 1960s the United Kingdom based Dunlop was one of the largest diversified multinationals, with some 60 percent of its revenue derived from overseas. The company traced its roots back to 1889 when John Dunlop and others formed a company to manufacture pneumatic bicycle tyres in Belfast. The company grew rapidly and factories for the manufacture of bicycle tyres were opened in the USA, France and Germany. Building on this capability, car tyres were manufactured from the early 1900s, followed by aeroplane tyres.

Over time the company pursued strategies to control key raw materials, owning rubber plantations in Ceylon and Malaya, and to control car tyre distributors. Geographic diversification continued with factories set up throughout the world. The company also diversified into the manufacture of golf balls and clubs, tennis balls and rackets, sports footwear and clothing, latex foam products, and a range of industrial products. Despite this, by the 1970s 60 percent of its revenue came from car tyres. The company suffered setbacks in the late 1960s due to poor management decisions in responding to: declining demand for tyres; the invention of technology that produced longer lasting tyres; competition from overseas producers; and the ill-fated merger with the Italian tyre company Pirelli.

In 1983 the company was the subject of a takeover and then broken up. Despite its long history of positioning for new opportunities, in the end key management failings included: confusing legacy products for core competencies; failure to shed poor performing tyre operations; and failure to adopt appropriate production processes, especially modern production technologies.

Introduction

Business angle focused businesses continually strive to find ways to work their way into new market opportunities. Businesses have to do this because markets are always in change, driven by, amongst other things, trends impacting customer expectations, the emergence of alternatives and the action of competitors. Businesses with core competencies and other resources have five paths that can be followed to parlay their position in the market into new business angles.

The purpose of this chapter is to describe ways businesses can leverage their core competencies into new opportunities in the market. This is more than the need for continuous improvement, it is the relentless drive for innovation in a business's place in the market. These are applications of Contributor 5 – valuable businesses reflecting the value of the scarce resources (see chapter 2 for the discussion on contributors).

The plan of this chapter is to start by explaining scarce resources, especially those developed by the capabilities of the business. These include how core competencies are identified, and how, having identified them, this knowledge can then be used to identify new business opportunities, or change the activity type, or reposition the business in the value network. This is a supply-side analysis, and viability would need to be addressed by incorporating information on market context. Following this there is discussion of each of the five paths to leverage core competencies. The final section discusses the implications for activity type and option premium.

Core competencies

Capabilities

There are many frameworks that seek to depict some or all of the key components of a business and the relationships between markets, outputs, production process and inputs, and the various stakeholders in such a way as to show how businesses differ from one another. Process and systems engineering have a practical interest in studying the relationship between capabilities and performance. This interest is to improve performance of production, inventory and logistics systems, and processes that can involve re-engineering entire systems in a value network. One technique used to depict these relationships is an adaption of process mapping, which relates outputs through capabilities to inputs. The contribution made by each capability can be assessed, compared to alternatives, and improved or replaced. These capabilities cover supporting back office capabilities as well as operational capabilities. Figure 17 depicts a stylised business's capabilities and their key interrelationships. The depiction is of a retail business using the arbitrage-arbitrage activity type, applying an organisational structure where capabilities are operated as distinct functional units, with formal communications between each unit. Note the division in the diagram of capabilities involved in product delivery and input acquisition methods, and that some capabilities straddle both areas.

Several capabilities are involved in the product delivery and input acquisition methods. Capabilities use knowhow, systems and processes to provide different attributes such as cost, quality and capacity. To achieve this, different production technologies are utilised, for example job, batch, flow systems and processes. To realise the objective of developing scarce resources, businesses have to invest in mechanisms to improve the likelihood of meeting plans and budgets by investing in capacity to enable business continuity. The overall management is provided by the organisational structure, which covers knowledge acquisition, business strategy, organisational architecture and incentive schemes.

Figure 17 Depiction of key capabilities and information flows of a simple retail merchant using arbitrage-arbitrage activity type operating in a functional organisational structure (applied to the product market perspective)

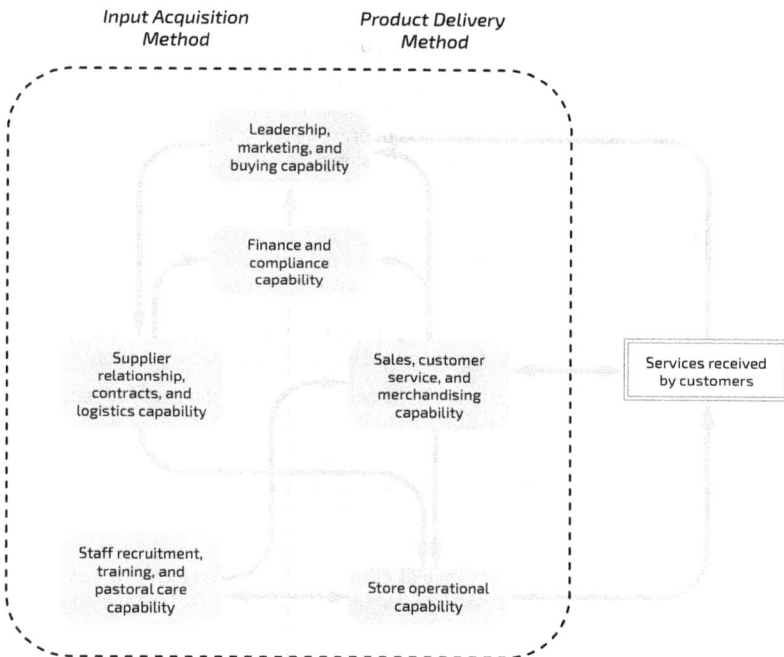

Types of capabilities

A capability consists of the capacity provided by knowhow, systems and processes to perform functional actions to deliver specified outputs, to execute risk mitigation actions to ensure business plans are realised, and to undertake actions to secure scarce resources by maintaining and enhancing their on-going income earning ability. Figure 18 is an influence diagram showing the key elements, and recursive and feedback loops that provide a representation of a capability. In this representation of the elements are: knowhow, systems and processes to perform actions and conditions (placed on nodes); and transactions and information flows (placed on arrows).

The influence diagram is read as follows: given the market context, the planned intervention products put into the market, underpinned by actions undertaken by the capabilities, in turn leads to financial results. No business operates as a simple linear model, as all are concerned about results and will respond by adjusting functional actions to improve results. In doing this all are also engaged in a range of risk mitigating actions. This is a set of actions utilised by a business to achieve their objectives within the constraints imposed by the financial position of the business. Risk mitigating actions cover a wide range of activities, including the use of various forms of insurance, development initiatives, as well as specific actions, whose purpose it is to reduce the cost of risk to the business. A crucial action is to preserve scarce resources. This action is frequently neglected, especially where there are constraints on funding. Examples of the omission of this action commonly found in business are underinvestment in: maintenance of resources, research to acquire new knowledge, and the continuous improvement of knowhow, systems and processes to reduce costs and improve quality.

These eight components, and four recursive and feedback loops, apply at a high level to each capability and the business as a whole. They also apply to each of the contributor markets in which the business operates. Figure 18 shows a perspective on the product market contributor of business opportunities. To place this in context of the discussion in chapter 2 on the sources of FCF value, this perspective is Contributor 1. Other perspectives are the supplier view and the shareholder view. In all these views the eight components will occur, although their content will be different. For complex modelling where the interactions across several perspectives are being considered, each contributor of business opportunities can form single modules in building the complex model. These models are complex because each view has at least four recursive/feedback loops (centred on the three sets of actions that are unique to the view and a common financial position).

The myriad ways in which actions can be performed have different impacts on the elements of the profit equation through the uncertainty premium.

Understanding these relationships is required for business planning, as the key variables that drive resourcing are identified in the influence diagram. The functionality is provided through the design of the knowhow systems and processes, and organisational structure of the business.

Figure 18 *Influence diagram of capabilities and four recursive/feedback loops to achieve the business's objectives (applied to the product market perspective)*

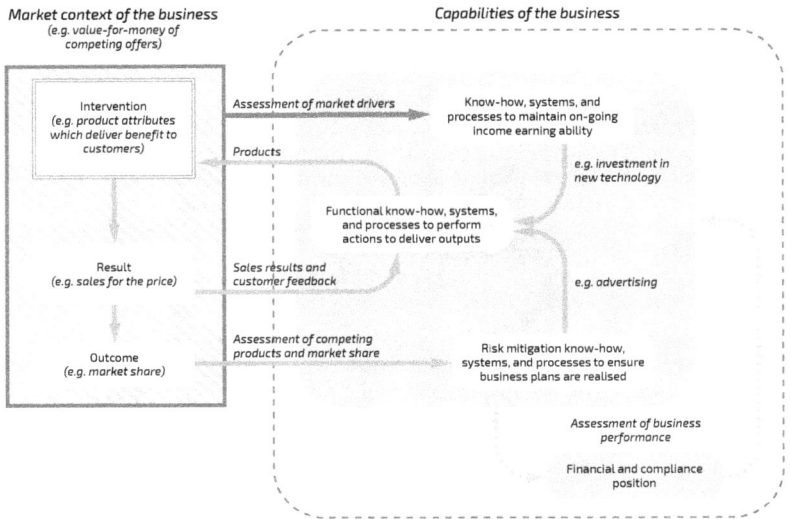

Organisational structure and capabilities

There is a wide and deep body of literature on the organisational structure of businesses and the choice of form. The range of organisational structures includes the traditional hierarchy, through to franchises, and the place and use of outsource contracts. Different organisational structures have different characteristics. Interest in alternative organisational structures has arisen because of the limitations of the hierarchical organisational structure in putting in place strong performance incentives and sanctions in many setting. This is particularly a problem in settings with coordination problems, where there are difficulties in finding providers, and it is difficult to clearly specify the product.

Organisational structure solves the internal coordination problem. It does this at a cost to the business, which is recouped from an improved FCF value of the business. Organisational structure influences capabilities in requiring functions to be performed, and placing constraints on the way all capabilities are performed and relate to one another. An organisational architecture that uses collaborative working practices and information sharing would have information flows to reflect those relationships, and would be different from those shown in Figure 17 (which is a functional organisational structure that operates each capability as a distinct management unit with formal communications between each unit). The scope of capabilities also varies between organisations operating the same activity type. This applies even where standardised systems and processes are used, such as accounting packages, as these are incorporated into the organisation in different ways. This is especially the case with businesses whose growth approach is to be led by actual sales made. These businesses continually parlay their most recent successes into new sales opportunities and this requires agility from the production process to respond to new opportunities.

Assessing whether capabilities are core competencies

Working out the alternative ways to leveraging existing resources relies on establishing the business's core competencies – that is to say its capabilities that are scarce resources. Whether a capability is a core competency rests on the degree to which a capability contributes to the objectives of the business. Where the capability does support the objectives of the business, then the next consideration is to compare the capability with the achievements of others to ascertain: whether the capability is available from alternative sources; and whether it is widely available to others. Where the capability is readily available in the market, then it may be possible to source information to assess the business's comparative performance in this capability. The next set of considerations explores the source of the competitive advantage provided by the capability, specifically whether the value is derived from accumulated experience or organisational wide knowhow, systems and processes. Here the interest is the routine and ongoing enhancement of the capability. A capability has the strongest case for being a core competency where it is valuable, rare, and costly to imitate because it is derived from accumulated experience and organisational wide knowhow, systems and processes. Where this is not the case, then the capability has lower potential for being core competency. For capabilities that meet this test only to some degree, then the best that can be said is that they possess the potential to be developed into a core competency, requiring further investment. Conversely, a core competency can lose this standing through competition or the business's own actions, which result in former core competencies no longer being valuable, rare and costly to imitate.

A process for identifying core competencies assesses each and every one of the business's capabilities. The result is an inventory of capabilities, with a rating of the degree to which each contributes to competitive advantage. This inventory and assessment of capabilities is also used to identify the actual activity type in operation within the business. Where management has a view on the planned activity type, then this assessment can indicate gaps in the current suite of competencies, and capabilities that are better acquired in other ways with the aim of improving competitive advantage. In extreme situations the assessment of core competencies may indicate that the activity type needs to be redesigned to better fit the market context, objectives of the business and available resources.

The capabilities of head offices and multidivisional businesses

The set of capabilities used by a business form the delivery and acquisition methods that give effect to the activity type used. Businesses with multiple lines of business are composed of several business angles. A business with multiple business lines could design the role of the head office with a business angle appropriate to that role. This would be fitting where the head office's attention has a strong focus on profiting from markets in contractual commitments and capital. The expectation here is that the head office will develop core competencies in capabilities - and associated activity type relevant to this role.

Paths to parlay a position in the market

New business angles can be opened up by using core competencies and other resources to create new business angles by:

- **Path 1** Positioning for new opportunities within a value network through integration, repositioning into more valuable places in the value network and expansion into allied value networks.
- **Path 2** Leveraging the initial market into a multi-sided market opportunity. This class of opportunity is available to some businesses operating in a part of the value network with high transaction costs.
- **Path 3** Extending the brand associated with the parent business angle.
- **Path 4** Applying scarce resources to different orders of market play.
- **Path 5** Realising through financial engineering improved market value in financial and asset markets.

A business development path involves the exploitation of one or more scarce resource. While the paths are not mutually exclusive, they may not be available to all businesses. Creating a multi-sided platform (Path 2) is more likely to be available to businesses with large customer bases. Businesses need to have a valuable brand to be able to benefit from brand extension opportunities (Path 3). They also require existing valuable scarce resources to be able to develop Path 4.

Path 1 — Positioning for new opportunities within a value network or allied value networks

Positioning for new opportunities within a value network is possibly the most common way that core competencies are leveraged. Five generic development strategies are used to launch initiatives to open up new business angles within a value network. These are:

- **Direction A** Growing market share. Where this encompasses merger and acquisition of other businesses with the same business angle it is horizontal integration.

- **Direction B** Expansion into allied markets, for example by adding new products. This exploits declining cost economies using existing activity type and core competencies.

- **Direction C** Changing the activity type through vertical integration with supplier and buyer stages of the value network.

- **Direction D** Changing the activity type to improve profit in current product markets.

- **Direction E** Expanding into new markets that require investment in new activity types, with the aim of repositioning at a higher value point in the value network.

For completeness, although not a development strategy, businesses can increase value by: withdrawing from some business angles with poor returns on market value; and the sale of assets that are worth more to others than the business.

The route to parlay a position in the market relies on a good understanding of current customers, markets for the supply of inputs, and activity types and their attendant knowhow, systems and processes, and organisational structure. At one level growing market share (Direction A) is doing more of the same, and increased size means additional capacity may need to be built and resourced. This may make the business more complex even though there is no change to the activity type. Similarly, expansion into allied markets (Direction B) may have no change to the activity type and additional capabilities required to support the increased product variety. But this is not always the case. Accessing new or increased market share may necessitate the adoption of a new activity type. A retailer may choose to expand retail presence by developing a franchise business model instead of, or in addition to, additional owned retail outlets.

Positioning for new opportunities in a value network involves changes to capabilities. Explicitly, changing the activity type that may extend to the use of mergers and acquisitions (Direction C) entails the addition of capabilities with the aim of building new competencies in the value network; and changing activity types to improve return on applied resources (Direction D) where there is no substantial change to products. Commonly this is seen in the move to outsource capabilities formerly undertaken in-house. It would be limiting to see this as a one way direction. Businesses also use outsourcing relationships in a number of ways, for example to build new capabilities that are then operated in-house by leapfrogging existing knowhow, systems and processes. In a sense, both these strategies are supply-side driven, in contrast to Direction E, which guides businesses to reposition to a different place in the value network to pursue new market opportunities, and with that, the need to develop a new business angle.

Direction A — Growth in the same market through horizontal integration

Growing market share is a strategy centred on exploiting a high level of knowledge of both markets and production processes. The economic justification for this strategy is the existence of positive feedback effects. A variant of this strategy is horizontal integration, where other businesses involved in the same business angle are acquired as a way to acquire additional capacity. Doing more of the same by refining a business model into the same market may well be the most widely used growth strategy. It is a strategy with limits imposed by the capacity constraints of the acquisition and delivery method capabilities. The capacity constraint is enterprise specific. For some there may not be an effective constraint, as the capabilities used by some internet business models are highly scalable even at very high transaction volumes.

Direction B — Growth into allied markets

The objective of expansion into allied markets is to take the core competencies created in one market into new markets by exploiting declining cost economies. These new markets can be in different geographic locations (horizontal integration) or even another industry, and for this new capabilities will need to be built.

Direction C — Growth through vertical integration

Changing the activity type through vertical integration with supplier and customer stages in the value network, in effect is changing the activity of the business. An example of this is vertical integration where, as an illustration, a manufacturing jeweller may open retail stores to provide certainty of distribution. This strategy would be pursued where there are net reductions in transaction costs between the two stages, and it involves developing or acquiring capabilities in the immediately preceding, or following, stages in the value network.

Direction D — Changing the activity type

This strategy changes the activity types while the product and its market remain unchanged. The effect of this is to reshape the cluster that may involve vertical integration with suppliers, or vertical disintegration by introducing new suppliers into the cluster. The adoption of an outsourcing method of acquiring products is not simply a change in the purchasing contract for an input, it requires the change of activity type. A change of activity type should be accompanied by redesigned production processes used by a business. Without this focus, this strategy could contribute to the continued demise of the business, as it attempts to stay in business by continuously cutting costs with no prospect of retaining core competencies.

Direction E — Reposition into more valuable places in the value network

Opportunities to reposition in a value network extend beyond simply bringing in-house capabilities, which were formerly undertaken by buyers and suppliers, to rearrange the allocation of capabilities within a cluster. Repositioning into more valuable places in the value network can be associated with the redrawing of the placement of capabilities within businesses and those businesses that make-up a cluster. When a business should take on capabilities from its buyers or suppliers through vertical integration arises where high transaction costs exist and savings are possible by using managerial arrangements rather than contractual arrangements. This is illustrated by the changes to value networks brought about by the logistics revolution. The logistics revolution has been a market disruption leading to significant reduction in costs in value networks achieved through improved coordination of delivery and lower inventories in the value network. To bring this about has required substantial innovation and investment in the capabilities that constitute the entire value network. The most noticeable result of this has seen truck transport reposition from an input service to manufacturers, to being an integral partner to manufacturers and distributors in gaining the benefits of integration and coordination. As an input, delivery was a cost to the manufacturer, frequently contracted under competitive supply arrangements. As a logistics partner these businesses improved the share of value added captured by manufacturers and distributors from the value network.

The core competency in positioning for new opportunities within a value network

Invariably the exploration of new opportunities that leverage existing competencies results in the need to develop new competencies, in order to open up new business angles; and in some settings this leads to the adoption of new activity types. For a business to repeatedly open up new sources of value from already developed core competencies, requires accumulated knowledge and experience in identifying new market opportunities, and in executing and putting in place an appropriate activity type. A variant of this development path is to collaborate with other businesses, so as to leverage the core competencies of the partners to develop new business angles.

Path 2 — Leveraging an initial market position into a multi-sided market

The opportunity to use an initial market position to create a multi-sided market opportunity is available to businesses that have developed scarce resources in a setting involving two or more groups of users. The prospects of this are strengthened where these groups face high shared transaction costs. The launch problem is reduced where the business operates in a part of the value network with high transaction costs. For businesses already operating an MSP+ there is the prospect of line-extending into new MSP+ opportunities.

Creating an MSP+ business angle by leveraging core competencies

The process to uncover MSP+ opportunities consists of identifying, for each product group, the fundamental sources of value-for-money to each customer group, in particular the ways that value-for-money are negatively impacted by high transaction cost. Having established this for the product group and its buyers, the business then needs to identify whether there are other groups with whom they frequently transact, and ascertain whether there are significant high transaction costs shared by the groups, that could be removed. The existence of shared transaction costs between at least two groups may provide an opportunity to design new systems and processes that reduce transaction costs between the customer groups. It also may provide opportunities to expand access of an existing product from one group to another, or to reduce the cost to launch new products by first launching to an existing customer group. How this process operates is illustrated with an example of a business raising finance. The funding process entails businesspeople presenting their case for funding to prospective backers. A significant hurdle faced by new businesspeople is trying to identify investors who would consider their proposal. The existence of two distinct user groups (businesspeople and investors), and high search costs, provides an opportunity for the creation of an MSP.

While all MSP+s have to deliver shared transaction costs savings, this is not the whole story, they also have to provide a high value proposition to all groups of users. The design of products with high product meaning is an essential way of achieving this. Product meaning refers to how buyers relate to a product because of positive connotations associated with its physical, functional, symbolic and cultural attributes. In saying this, it is not sufficient to offer products with high product meaning without also providing high value-for-money. High product meaning is especially pertinent where there are competing products readily available. MSP+ products deliver high shared transaction costs savings to users through products with product meaning, and which offer high value-for-money.

MSPs occur at any point in a value network and are one of two types: receiver-sender platforms linking suppliers and buyers; or peer-to-peer platforms linking members within a group. Receiver-sender platforms at the final consumption stage in a value network are market places, shopping malls, information discovery services such as real estate listings, and communications networks such as the postal service. Receiver-sender platforms at input supply stages in the value network are market places such as trade shows, information discovery services such as job boards, and communications networks. Peer-to-peer platforms also exist in the provision of information discovery and communications networks. Examples from the final consumption stage in a value network are, respectively, introduction sites and social media. A peer-to-peer platform at the input supply stages in a value network is, for example, a payment system. Note that in many of these examples, the platform does not restrict its activities to only one position in the value network or a single type of transaction.

There are several reasons a full range of product types are offered on MSPs. The first is the competition from disintermediation from direct supply between the parties and resellers who seek to own the customer relationship – these are examples of business opportunities that are created by the existence of MSPs. Another reason is that the volume of transactions on a large MSP can generate significant declining cost economies. In addition, the volume of transactions on large MSPs generates data on user behaviours, which can be used to further reduce operating costs, remove shared transaction costs and identify opportunities for new applications products.

Leveraging an existing customer base

The outstanding fact in the creation of valuable MSP+s is the need to solve the chicken-and-egg problem of getting enough parties on to the platform to achieve critical mass. Launch is a severe problem for potential MSP+s with the vast majority of new to market initiatives failing, including those by businesses with experience in growing MSP+s. Key factors that appear to increase the chances of gaining critical mass are: having a high value proposition to both groups of users, launching into an existing group who value the new offering, and retaining focus on those in the new group having strongest shared transaction costs with the initial user base. Launching into an existing group can significantly increase the likelihood of success of launching a new MSP offering. The ramification of this is introducing the new product as an extension to the current product, rather than a separate unrelated new product. Without using the existing MSP+, reaching critical mass can be an insurmountable problem, a problem exacerbated in small markets. Launching into an existing group can so significantly improve the likelihood of success of launching a new MSP+ product, that for businesses already operating a successful MSP+, the existence of groups enjoying strong cross-group effects is their single most valuable resource.

Leveraging positive cross-group effects

Strong positive cross-group effects dramatically increase the profitability of a business angle. It is in this way that their existence, and continued maintenance and enhancement, represent a scarce resource in the same way that brand value is viewed. MSPs are made more valuable by strengthening positive cross-group effects. This requires continual refinement of the offered value propositions. Many markets exhibit cross-group effects where a more extensive product range attracts more customers. With higher sales, it becomes more attractive to offer a comprehensive range of products.

Value network arbitrage opportunities exist where the product derived from information from one group of users (in one value network) is of interest to a separate group of users (in another value network). For there to be value in this, information asymmetries of knowledge between groups of users must exist. Amongst buyers for the information there must be low ability to share information. This could be because the information is not of universal interest or the interest is idiosyncratic. Opportunities to source this information are often from businesses engaged in transaction processing and network industries.

Because MSP+s insert themselves in a value network to facilitate transactions between parties, disintermediation is a threat to platform operators. Disintermediation refers to transacting parties bypassing the platform and dealing directly with one another. To guard against this, platforms have to ensure they are removing, and continue to focus on removing, significant shared transaction costs from the market that the parties would face when operating outside the platform.

There are a number of competitive strategies used in markets with strong positive cross-group effects including multi-homing, providing full interoperable compatibility with the dominant player then cherry-picking the market, and maintaining platform incompatibility. Multi-homing refers to a situation where competing offers operate alongside one another, with users signing up to competing offers showing no particular preference for any of the alternatives. The most well-known example of multi-homing is credit cards. The aim of a multi-homing strategy for platform providers is to split the market for transactions. For example with two major credit card companies, each will have a share of the available transactions. In contrast, providing full interoperable compatibility with the dominant player provides the competitor the opportunity to cherry-pick the market for high value customers. The aim of this strategy is to try to get the dominant player to behave as if they were operating in a single-sided market, and competing in a single market neglecting the second sides of the market and their feedback effects. The third competitive strategy is to maintain platform incompatibility. The aim of this strategy is to segment the market. The reward from this strategy is from the sale of content such as apps, music, videos and games that are not available on the other platforms. This strategy is an option where the market is large enough to support several competing MSPs.

Competitors who succeed in splitting a market may reduce the market share faced by each platform operator below critical mass, eliminating any advantage from positive feedback effects. A market disrupting business angle could undermine the revenue model of an existing MSP. An example is the revenue model of newspapers based on classified advertisements, which was disrupted by auction websites and search engines.

Line extending an existing MSP+

MSP+s are like other business opportunities and their core competencies can be leveraged into new opportunities. In particular, they are able to parlay their customer bases as a way to stimulate cross-group effects. Businesses operating in markets subject to positive cross-group effects are on a knife edge, in that positive cross-group effects operate to different strengths on the different parties, and the strength can change with circumstances. Circumstances, serendipity and the strength of the cross-group effects can see a single business pull ahead, and others losing market share.

Path 3 — Brand extension as a way to grow new business angles

Brand extension opportunities arise from the positive notoriety associated with a business's existing products. Brand extension opens up new revenue opportunities, while at the same time it can also reinforce the brand of the parent product. The ability to create brand is frequently associated with positive feedback effects for the parent product, increasing demand for it.

All established products have an element of brand image that is integral to the identity of the business that supplies it – in some cases this is no more than the location of the supplier. In other cases it is much more than this and a brand image is a part of product meaning. The possibility of creating brand occurs in markets where products experience positive notoriety, such as fashion trends. It is this notoriety that is leverage into new business angles. The ability to create brand notoriety is a fundamental business activity.

Brand meaning is a component of the consumer experience of a product. Elements of brand can be legally protected in the form of trademarks. In some cases laws that create property rights enable the trade in the ownership of brands. Having said this, enforcement of these rights can be expensive and can be challenged. Brand meaning can also be lost, for example, because of ill-conceived actions of the brand owner. The creation of legal rights is of little consequence if they are not monetised in some way to create a positive or enhance an existing income stream. Two forms of brand extension are found: simulacra and brand stretching into allied markets.

Simulacra

Simulacra are brand extension opportunities that involve the creation of a hyper-reality surrounding the brand. There are well-known examples of businesses that have developed new simulacra, initially inspired by fictional characters in book series, comic books, cartoon film characters, celebrities and sport teams. The simulacra can be themed tours and parks, and merchandising. Simulacra business angles are compatible with the parent market proposition but are quite different in their new manifestation, for example, comic books and their simulacra as films. In most cases this difference is so substantial that simulacra require new business angles whose competencies are not derived from those of the parent business angle. This is so much the case that there are businesses whose business angle is to monetise the creations of simulacra opportunities.

As simulacra create a hyper-reality that is rooted in the parent product, arguably any compromise to its brand value would undermine the simulacra product and vice versa. Simulacra that create new business angles require development of new competencies. In addition, because of the close relationship between the parent product and its hyper-reality manifestation, there is benefit in also having a capability to ensure the consistent management of the brand, and to ensure that the brand remains difficult to replicate. To achieve this, a variety of legal protections are utilised, such as copyright and design protections. This capability's aim is to preserve the resource's value to the owner, and ensure that it is not inadvertently damaged by the business's own actions.

Brand stretching as a source of cost advantage

In this setting brand stretching does not involve the creation of a hyper reality, instead it capitalises on attributes such as recognition, quality, and trust in the parent brand by extending them to new products. The economic drivers underlying this are derived from reduced advertising costs and increased product attribute benefits. These two factors are formidable and underpin second mover strategies, businesses with strong brands that enter a market that has been opened up and proven by an innovator.

Brand has significant economic benefits that can make the need for a capability to protect it worthwhile. One economic benefit attributed to brand is the reduction in promotion costs when applied to other products. Brand stretching is also associated with the transfer of quality attributes to products, and in this way increasing value-for-money. Strong brands can give such a strong advantage so as to create second mover advantage. Second mover advantage applies to markets where an innovative pioneer does the work to prove the value of a product, which is then entered by a strong brand holder able to gain a cost advantage over the incumbent, and in some cases, force the innovator out of the market.

The activity types to exploit a perceived opportunity from brand extension are different from those of the parent business angle. The selection of activity type follows the process described earlier. Businesses exploiting brand in this manner benefit from having capabilities to ensure the various business angles exploiting the brand do so in a manner that is both consistent with the image of brand, and provides the greatest opportunities for positive feedback between the business angles, so as to further enhance the brand.

Path 4 — The application of scarce resources to create different orders of market play

Another way to leverage scarce resources into new business angles is to apply them in an unrelated market. For most businesses, the proposition is that core competencies from one business angle can provide new insights into new business opportunities in quite different markets. This path is seen in operation where several businesses collaborate to innovate and create new core competencies for new market opportunities. Collaboration of this type is an effective way to reduce and share the cost of uncertainty, particularly where the pace of change and complexity is high. This development path can lead to the development of innovations capable of driving significant change in markets.

The application of core competencies to create different orders of market play is an important development path for businesses, as markets are primed for change. They are primed for change because businesspeople are ever alert to opportunities for speculation. The search for an angle on a business opportunity is on-going, which further destabilises the market. This is particularly the case because market instability opens up new opportunities, such as instability resulting from technological change, innovation of new products, uncertainty, mispricing and other errors. Market stability can attract interest from parties whose specific interest is to find and take to market business propositions to disrupt markets.

This is not a level playing field, with businesses having equal access to the benefits from opportunities. Market change is also brought about by serendipity and positive feedback effects that have different impacts – partly because of the different activity types that are being used. These positive feedback effects include demand-side effects (such as social network effects) and supply-side effects (such as declining cost economies). The impact of change and imperfection on a business's growth and success is that positive feedback effects on small random changes result in market growth for some businesses, at the expense of others. A consequence is that industry concentration increases over time with some businesses growing to dominate the market.

In addition to the behaviour of market participants that cause the weight of flow of money to change, there are significant external factors that introduce instability into markets. These include shocks to markets, for instance the Global Financial Crisis of 2007 was an event that fell outside of most business's expectations. Here too, the possibility of unexpected market behaviour also presents business opportunities. It should be added that offsetting these sources of instability, are sources of inertia in the market, for example, those imposed by regulatory and institutional arrangements, monopoly power, tight clustering in value networks, and institutional rigidities.

Even where the collaboration of businesses leads to profitable outcomes, there is no certainty that the partners will benefit equally. This could be because one of the coalition members involved in bringing about the change may end up appropriating the value added. This might occur where the innovation is based on a new scarce product from a supplier, as yet unproven in the market. Success of this product in this application could open up new market opportunities for it, and now being a scarce resource with increased demand, the product owner could capture the available value added.

Once a market is in change, then there are two facets to consider. One is that market instability represents opportunities for new entrants, and the other is that market instability increases uncertainty making picking winners more difficult. Rapid change in a market attracts market participants eager to share in the flow of money. For example, in growth markets this can be 'developers' launching new ventures into the market, or in declining markets businesses becoming takeover targets to be stripped of assets.

Path 5 — Opportunities associated with financial and asset markets

From the financial market's standpoint, businesses allocate and manage capital. A measure of a business's success in this mission is growth in market value. But this is not a simple measure to interpret, as a change in value is due to a variety of factors, specifically: a general expansion or contraction in value of the economy, a change in outlook for the entire industry, a change in the demand for ownership interest in the business, and the particular strategic choices and operational decisions of management. The significance of growing value goes well beyond gauging how well this mission has been fulfilled, and the contribution of each of these factors has to be accounted for. Growth in value captures both the quantity of value growth, and the overall quality of resource management in the setting of the various other factors that impact on market value. While there are countless individual things that managers can do to create value, they all fall into one of three types of strategies. Value increases where: the return earned on scarce resource already employed is improved (that is, if more profits are generated without tying up any more resource); additional resource is invested in projects or strategies that more than cover the option premium; and resources are withdrawn from activities that produce inadequate return.

Financial assets can be located in each of the element markets in which a business operates. This can be illustrated using the value of the business to owners. Financial markets on the other hand present several avenues to harvest the value of a business, including: by making the business more valuable through reducing transaction costs, barriers to entry, barriers to access, difficulty in assessing risk, in the following ways, for example:

- Making assets more marketable. This might require making the asset more marketable by changing its form of ownership, for example, through listing on an exchange.
- Realising the value by identifying and disposing of assets worth more to others than the business, for example, securitising loan books.
- Improving value by identifying and withdrawing from business angles with poor returns on market value.
- Improving market value through identifying opportunities from change in asset use that increases the value of assets.
- Selling/buying back of equity, that is selling when demand increases and price is high, and buying back when demand decreases and price is low.

Value locked up in a business can also be released by splits and leveraging, for example by:

- Improving market value through identifying opportunities for splitting of elements of the assets into separate securities, which are valuable to others.
- Sourcing funds by leveraging assets as security for lending.
- Identifying the basis of a new business, for instance whereby extending unsecure retail credit, a finance business is created.

Business value can also be realised by participating in the creation of portfolios, such as those created by facilitating industry consolidation, particularly when driven by the need to gain the benefits of declining cost economies to compete internationally.

Business angles to pursue opportunities associated with financial asset markets are created using each of the activity types, and develop core competencies. In most cases the value network of these businesses intersects with other businesses in other value networks, through their participation in financial asset markets.

Summary

There are five paths through which assets and resources created by core competencies are leveraged into new opportunities. The most commonly used of these paths, Path 1, repositions with a value network or uses existing core competencies to enter allied new markets. Positioning for new opportunities within a value network is by: vertical integration; repositioning into more valuable places in the value network; and horizontal integration, which could change the activity type. Two of the paths do not change the parent business angle, instead they create new business angles from the assets and resources of the parent business angle. Each of these new business angles is supported by a new activity type. These new business angles are associated with adding new markets, first, where there are strong cross-group effects associated with the parent business angle in the form of multi-sided markets (Path 2) and, second, by exploiting economies associated with brand (Path 3). Businesses that exploit brand in this way have a specific capability to nurture and care for brands as a valuable asset. One of the paths (Path 4) uses scarce resources to pursue new market opportunities at different orders of market play, and for this new business angles are developed using new activity types. A fifth path is also identified, which is focused on realising value through financial engineering, improved market value in financial and asset markets. Businesses actively engaged in this aspect of commerce are likely to have dedicated capabilities.

The development paths for existing core competencies are set out in Figure 19. The key take-away lesson from this table is that a business, which has developed core competencies to support a business angle, has a number of different ways to leverage these into new business angles.

Figure 19 *Development paths for existing core competencies*

Parent activity type	Parent market opportunity		
	Unchanged	*Unchanged with the addition of new business angles (with supporting activity type) in new markets*	*Changed (breaking with the past)*
Unchanged	**Path 1** Growth in the same market, for example by exploiting knowledge of specific perceived opportunities in the market.	**Path 2** Developing multi-sided markets. Path 3 Creating new assets in the form of brand extension. There is also likely to be a capability to manage the brand as a corporate asset. Path 5 Realising value from capital and asset markets.	**Path 1** Growth into allied markets.
Changed	**Path 1** A new position in the value network by changing the boundary of the business.		**Path 4** Moving to different orders of market play. This involves new activity types.

Selected literature review

Early origin of idea

The central ideas of profit and value of scarce resources that underpin comparative advantage were developed by David Ricardo in *On the Principles of Political Economy and Taxation* published in 1817.

Key influences on the work

A key writer on core competencies and their value to a business is Barney, for example the 2001 article 'Is the resource-based 'view' a useful perspective for strategic management research? Yes' published in *Academy of Management Review*. The interpretation used here is drawn from Black and Boal in 'Strategic Resources: Traits, Configurations and Paths to Sustainable Competitive Advantage' a paper in the *Strategic Management Journal of 1994*.

The application of inference diagrams is described in texts on systems theory. Inference diagrams and general systems theory have been widely applied to understanding business problems. See for example Maani and Cavana *Systems Thinking and Modelling: Understanding Change and Complexity* published by Pearson Education New Zealand in 2000. The use of inference diagrams to understand the impact of risk on organisations is described in a 2011 Queen Mary University of London paper by Fenton and Neil *The use of Bayes and causal modelling in decision-making, uncertainty and risk*.

SEVEN
Changing business angles by removing friction from the value network

From its start, telecommunications dramatically reduced transaction costs faced by businesses. Within little more than twenty years of Samuel Morse inventing and testing the two wire telegraph and Morse Code, in 1838, there were thousands of kilometres of telegraph. This trend was reinforced by the development of a transatlantic undersea cable in 1866. Landline telecommunications was ubiquitous by the mid Twentieth Century. Wireless telecommunications was a key early part of the development of telecommunications. A significant milestone was the demonstration in 1901 by Marconi of transatlantic wireless communications. Consumer landline and wireless communications converged with the commercialisation by Motorola, in the early 1970s, of the mobile phone. By the end of the Twentieth Century mobile phones were in common use.

In comparison computer systems are a much more recent innovation, only appearing in commercial applications in the early 1960s where they were mainly used to support business processes. Increased use saw developments in operating systems and programming languages. Among the significant developments in the 1970s were virtual machine operating systems and the emergence of personal computers. The use of computers in business increased substantially with the introduction of the IBM PC in 1981, reinforced by developments in graphical user interfaces, popularised in particular by Apple. Since then personal computers have gone onto become commonplace in businesses and homes, and as mobile personal computing devices.

The use of telecommunications networks through a computer network occurred early on, demonstrating the potential to further reduce transaction costs faced by businesses. The most notable of these was the 1960s airline booking system SABRE. Developments in packet switching from 1960 to the 1980s that underpin the internet, and protocols linking hypertext documents in the 1980s, provided the foundation for the World Wide Web. Telecommunications companies offered Virtual Private Network services in the 1990s and provided the backbone for the rollout of the internet. With increased use of the internet transaction costs began to reduce rapidly. Developments in cloud computing since 2000, and mobile computing supported by cheap hand-held devices, reinforced the development of new products and business models that further drove down transaction costs for parties communicating over the internet.

These developments have also driven down the capital investment requirements for business processes. The emergence of software-as-a-service (SaaS) enables businesses to simply pay providers for the use of systems and processes as a service accessed through the internet rather than the business having to own, operate and maintain copies of the software, servers and supporting networks and peripheral devices. These developments reduced the barriers to entry and operating costs for the use of sophisticated ICT systems and processes. A wide range of new businesses have emerged to take advantage of these developments.

Introduction

Multi-sided platforms and market places can provide great benefit to businesses in terms of improved access to markets. The flip side to this is that it does so for all businesses on the platform. MSPs give small businesses the same access to buyers as large businesses, potentially undermining any advantages from size, strong brand or investment in distribution channels. MSPs also reduce barriers to entry for new entrants. MSPs illustrate a more general case of reduced transaction costs between suppliers and their buyers, making it more conducive for businesses to buy in products rather than produce them in-house. Better access to markets increases the addressable market but comes with increased competition. The big winner from reduction in transaction costs is buyers.

Reductions in transaction costs trigger changes in market structure, the capabilities undertaken within businesses, and the structure of the entire value network. In accommodating the new conditions in the market, businesses transition from one activity type to another. By parlaying their position in the market, hybrid activity types are developed and business angles are evolved. This is a dynamic process of changing capabilities to support the product set offered by the business, which too is changing as the market changes. The value network adapts to realise economic advantages within the available capital and risk bearing for the potential return. Different business angles follow different market trajectories, and changing the business angle changes the trajectory a business follows in the market.

To maintain profits, within the constraints faced by owners, businesses need to continuously align the business angle to market conditions by adjusting the place in the value network and activity type used. This is especially necessary where transaction costs are falling. This chapter also explores the strategies available to businesses to position in a value network. Five strategies are identified. The approach taken in this chapter is first to explain the impact of transaction costs in shaping the structure of the value network. This is followed by a discussion of the impact of reduced transaction costs on the choice of place in the value network and activity type. The range of market positioning strategies is then discussed.

The impact of transaction costs on the capabilites of the business

Transaction cost

That the activity types of businesses are matched to the nature of markets is a widely accepted idea. By understanding the nature of the product required, a buyer determines the most appropriate supply arrangement to employ. There are a range of possible supply arrangements between buyers and suppliers. These include: none, with the buyer owning the resource to deliver the product internally, forming a joint venture with other resource owners for the production of a product, through to establishing a preferred supplier relationship, or simply negotiating a contract for supply with a supplier. In selecting the most appropriate supply arrangement for a product, the buyer will wish to minimise the combined cost of locating and negotiating with a supplier, the cost of the product, and the cost of administering the supply arrangement. Suppliers also seek to minimise the cost of marketing, sales, and to serve customers. Specifically, the costs involved in transacting are due to:

- The costs incurred to specify the requirement, search and locate potential suppliers, evaluate supply arrangements, and contract to acquire the product.
- The frequency with which the product is acquired.
- Whether the products have specifications unique to the customer's requirements and have no alternative use.
- The availability of alternatives and intensity of competition among potential suppliers.
- The ease with which performance of the supplier can be assessed.
- The degree of uncertainty involved in acquiring the desired product, for example whether technical innovation is involved.
- The cost to the buyer of risk of non-performance by the supplier.
- The effect of information transfer to a supplier (that is, potential loss of competitive advantage or possible dependency on one supplier).

In evaluating alternatives a buyer considers market context, for instance, whether there are established suppliers of the product and the degree of competition in the market. In markets with many equal size buyers and suppliers of a standardised product there is low dependence between suppliers and buyers. Either party can switch with little net loss. The extent to which the product is contract specific is a consideration in determining the appropriate supply arrangement. As a general guideline, where contract specific investment required to supply a product is low, many businesses would compete to offer the product. In such situations, purchasing the product on the open market has an advantage over producing it internally. This is because suppliers in a competitive market have stronger incentives to perform than could be placed on staff employed to do the work internally. If an external supplier in a competitive market fails to perform, it is easy for the buyer to end the relationship and find another supplier. It is generally more difficult to close down an internal operation. Dependence on a supplier is even lower with low barriers to entry - small and medium size businesses could compete without disadvantage, with very strong incentives to perform as the threat of losing sales would be real.

In the opposite situation, where very significant resource investment must be made, it is likely that only a few large suppliers will be able to compete to provide the product. When competition is significantly restricted, it is preferable to own and manage the resources to deliver the product in-house. This is because as competition reduces, so do the incentives for performance. In this situation the external supplier knows that, in the case of failure to perform, it is very difficult for the buyer to end the contract and replace it with another. A high degree of dependence can develop between the buyer and supplier. The development of highly specialist, or contract specific, software is a good example of this. Open markets do not function well when dependency develops.

Between these two extremes are many cases where the level of contract specific investment is considered intermediate. In these situations buyers cannot rely on the threat of competition to provide all the incentives necessary to ensure good performance. Longer-term contracts with specified performance standards and default provisions, or franchise relationships with appropriate sanctions, are among the preferred contracting options.

Two main conclusions flow from this. In highly competitive markets there are very strong incentives on external suppliers to perform. In such situations the costs of managing suppliers, and monitoring their performance, are low. Conversely, when there is little threat of competition, the incentives for performance are low, and the costs of managing and monitoring suppliers are high. As the resource investment required to deliver a product increases, the intensity of competition decreases. When the investment required is small, contracting with external suppliers is the preferred relationship. When major contract specific investment is required, however, it is more suitable to own and manage the resource internally. In an intermediate situation, longer-term contracts, or relationships such as joint ventures are appropriate.

In relationships between buyers and suppliers opportunistic behaviour is a possibility. The objective of the buyer is to ensure close alignment of suppliers to their interests. There are a number of ways of aligning the interests of a supplier to these of the buyer. These include using incentives and sanctions, close monitoring and formal contracts. Each of these methods imposes costs on the parties. These costs rise according to the extent of divergence between the interests of the supplier and those of the buyer.

Where there are substantial problems in monitoring and/or measuring the performance of suppliers, it is more efficient to manage production in-house, rather than contracting them out. Generally speaking, it is more efficient for a business to contract work out than to perform it internally, when: the buyer is able to monitor the performance of external suppliers; the cost of measuring supplier performance is not out of proportion to the cost of delivering the product; the risk of failure to perform is low, in other words, if an external supplier fails to perform the ongoing survival of the buyer is not threatened; and, large investments in contract specific resources are not required.

Having established the conditions determining the nature of the contract to be used in the purchase transaction, these conditions also apply to the question of who should own a resource. The ownership of a resource is determined by which party has the strongest incentives to increase the resource's value.

The existence of transaction costs is one of the reasons that a range of activity types exist. The other reasons are sources of economies, and the existence of limitations on access to information and knowledge to interpret that information.

Outsourcing in response to reduction in transaction costs

As a general statement, a market that faces a reduction in transaction costs sees increased use of purchasing arrangements to acquire products and less use made of in-house production. This will apply to any buyer-supplier arrangement. Suppliers able to remove transaction costs on their products accompany this with a simpler supply contract. In the face of reduction in transaction costs, businesses prefer to acquire more capabilities under contract rather than performing them internally. This also applies to investment, to put in place distribution channels, for instance through the use of franchise arrangements. Businesses are able to reduce the transaction costs on their products, and in that way the use of markets to acquire products, by:

- Reducing the costs incurred in acquiring the product.
- Increasing the frequency with which the product is required.
- Reducing the contract specificity of the product.
- Making it easy to assess supplier performance.
- Improving the degree of certainty involved in delivering to a specification.
- Reducing the cost to the buyer, of non-performance by the supplier.
- Reducing the impact of information transfer from the buyer to the supplier.

Buyers or suppliers are able to take the initiative to reduce transaction costs in order to facilitate the use of competitive market supply arrangements.

The impact of transaction costs on the value network

Market positioning strategies

To find a place in a market, a business needs transaction costs to be lower than internal supply, and to apply one of five positioning strategies:

- **Position 1** Cost advantage where the business has a low average cost structure, compared to competitors, achieved through choice of activity type and place in the value network, and ability to supply products at a lower unit price for equivalent benefits than competitors.
- **Position 2** Local advantage where the lower cost to a supplier of reaching local buyers is exploited.
- **Position 3** Extemporaneous advantage stemming from conditions where buyers are willing to pay a premium because of a product's availability at the right time and place.
- **Position 4** Segmentation advantage where the attributes of the product are changed so as to provide a targeted sub-group of buyers with better value-for-money than competing products.
- **Position 5** Transaction cost advantage gained from removing shared transaction costs from parties wishing to transact with one another.

Relative bargaining power determines the allocation of value added

The allocation of value added between two stages in a value network is determined by the relative bargaining power of the parties involved. This can be illustrated by using capacity constraints on suppliers to meet demand as a lever to increase their bargaining power.

Suppose the prevailing market price for a product is known, and the highest price providers could charge without attracting investment such as new entrants into the market is also known. This upper price (P_U) may be discovered from industry experience where there appears to be a glass ceiling to the profit margin achievable before new entrants (frequently from other geographic localities) are attracted into the market. While the perceived benefit to buyers is above this price, a price above this is unattainable by suppliers without attracting more competitors into the market. This portrayal of a market with relatively few suppliers requiring lumpy investment is a realistic depiction of many markets in which the effective competition is from relatively few suppliers (commonly competitor analysis involves three or four larger businesses and seven or so smaller identifiable competitors).

A method of calculating the allocation of value added where there are few suppliers and/or buyers is described in this section. In practice the use of this method requires detailed understanding of the competitive structure of a market including product pricing and benefit attributes which is feasible where there are relatively few competitors involved in a market. By making some simplifying assumptions the following sections explore the operation of the five positioning strategies.

The initial scenario is a competitive market which, for simplicity, has many similar buyers, and three similar providers (called A, B and C), where there are no constraints on buyers finding providers or in the capacity to supply. Starting with aggregate demand by buyers and providers who can individually supply the entire demand, the providers have no bargaining power, as a buyer can select the provider or providers able to supply all their requirements at the lowest price (P_L). Each buyer retains the entire available value added, which is P_U, the maximum available to providers, less P_L, the lowest supply price. Providers can lay claim to none of the available value added.

Figure 20 shows this situation. The supply curve is the straight horizontal line at the price of P_L, extending past the demand curve, as suppliers have more capacity than there is demand. For simplicity it is a highly price inelastic aggregate demand curve, so there is no meaningful change in sales between the upper and lower limit prices. Relaxing this condition would see a change in price being associated with a change in the quantity demanded such that as price increases the demand falls and vice versa. Price can be an effective instrument to constrain demand.

The situation changes where there are capacity constraints and providers are unable to supply the entire need of buyers. Introducing a constraint in the supply capacity puts providers in a position where they are able to share in the available value added. It is a matter of bargaining power how this value is actually allocated between buyers and providers, and the price is struck between P_L and P_U, the lower and upper bound prices. This is the straight horizontal line supply curve intersecting with the y-axis at P_S in Figure 20. The greater the capacity constraint the closer the supply price will be to the upper bound price – the point at which new entrants will come into the market. Capacity constraints are a frequent occurrence in markets. It is especially prevalent in industries with a high cyclical component such as building and construction.

Figure 20 *Demand and supply curves illustrating the allocation of value added between buyers and providers being determined by relative bargaining power*

The general observations from this initial scenario are:

- Capacity constraint in meeting demand is a key factor in increasing the bargaining power of providers.
- The price that attracts new investment into a market provides the upper limit to price that incumbent producers can charge.

Using this initial scenario, the discussion turns now to each of the positioning strategies.

Position 1 — Strategies based on cost advantage

Adopting a cost advantage strategy a producer (A) aims to supply products at a lower cost, for equivalent benefits, than competitors. For this discussion the cost structure of A is less than those of competitor B, which in turn is less than those of C. This situation is represented in demand and supply graphs in Figure 21. A makes sales up to its capacity constraint, followed by B, and finally C provides the balance. The highest cost provider able to find a place in the market sets the market price at its supply cost, which in this illustration is set by producer C. Producer A captures value added equal to the difference between the market price set by producer C and its supply cost, similarly B captures value added of the difference between the market price and its supply cost.

The removal of transaction costs for all suppliers shifts the supply curve down. Reducing transaction costs does not change the allocation of value added between the providers.

With excess capacity in the market, removing transaction costs from the entire market increases demand; with the inefficient supplier gaining increased sales from this. Achieving a cost leadership position is a robust market positioning strategy in the face of declining transaction costs.

Where overall capacity is insufficient to meet demand, the removal of transaction costs faced by all buyers may result in no reduction in price because providers bargaining power increases and, therefore, the value added captured by each provider increases. The balance here is whether increased profit margin is sufficient to attract new investment in capacity.

Figure 21 *Demand and supply curves showing the impact of change in transaction cost on the allocation of value added*

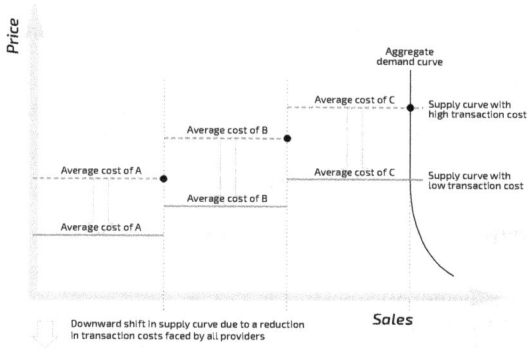

Position 2 — Strategies based on local advantage

In a competitive market with local producers facing no transaction cost and other producers facing high transaction cost, high cost local providers can remain in the market. A common situation where these conditions exist is found in small local businesses that local buyers can more easily buy from. There may also be an element of preference in dealing with local suppliers, a situation discussed in Position 4.

Demand and supply curves are presented in Figure 22. If C is the local producer with no transaction costs, and A and B face transaction costs which make them more costly than A, then the order in which sales are met is first by allocating capacity to the lowest price product, then allocating capacity to successively higher priced products which are from the local producer C, followed by A and B. Price will be set by B and the transaction cost. With the removal of transaction costs, C is revealed to be a high cost producer and sales are met first by A, followed by B and residual provided by C. C now sets the price. The impact of the removal of transaction costs is to improve total market value added and undermine local advantage.

Figure 22 *Demand and supply curves showing the impact of local advantage and high transaction cost on other suppliers*

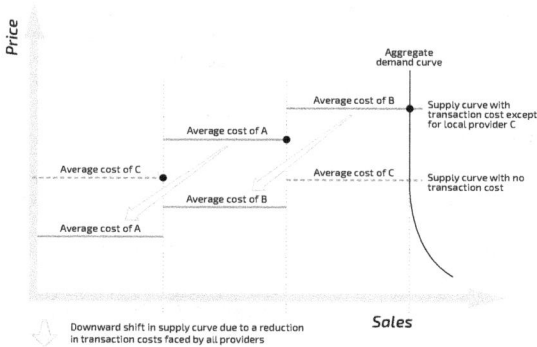

Position 3 — Strategies based on extemporaneous advantage

Extemporaneous advantage arises from conditions where buyers are willing to pay a premium because of the product's availability at the right time and place. For buyers, these opportunities are characterised by their high transaction costs, for instance in identifying alternative potential suppliers. On the one hand this is a situation where businesses that have invested in buyer specific relationships would wish to maintain, as it excludes potential competitors. On the other hand, providers without this investment could gain from reduced transaction costs. What is taken from this is that extemporaneous advantage is highly susceptible to being undermined by reduction in transaction costs.

Position 4 — Strategies based on value-for-money advantage

Value-for-money advantage enables the provider to segment the market. This is at a lower or higher price point than that provided by others in the market. Figure 23 shows a situation where differentiation is based on buyers willing to pay a higher price for the unique, higher benefits associated with the product with benefit b. Creating this type of market niche is a high cost market position to sustain, as it requires investment to segment a market to create and maintain barriers to entry. Segmentation can also be achieved by offering lower quality at a commensurate lower price to improve value-for-money. This is the product with benefit a. Where the product offers dramatic value-for-money improvement at a lower price it could disrupt the market (for example a product with benefit b offered at the price of the product with benefit a).

Where supplier C is able to supply product b at a price lower than P_b it will be able to sell up to its supply capacity. The supply curve would be stepped with C supplying up to its capacity constraint (shown on the right hand side of the supply curve) and with the most efficient producer of product with benefits a (producer A) supplying up to its capacity constraint (shown on the left hand side of the supply curve). The remaining capacity is supplied by B, a producer of product a. The price of product a is B's cost of supply. The investment in capacity to produce product b by C will depend on the price elasticity of demand for b and the cross price elasticity of demand between products b and a. Investment will take place up to the point that marginal cost of the new capacity equals the marginal revenue from product b.

The ability to capture part of the available value added through segmentation can be estimated. Where a provider segments the market by supplying superior benefits, then providers increase their access to the available value added. In the example shown in Figure 23, C supplies a product that offers superior benefit b, but at a higher cost. Also available in the market is another product offering the same value-for-money, but with lower benefit a, and at a lower price. There are no supply constraints in the supply of product a.

Where a provider segments the market by supplying higher value-for-money to buyers, but at constrained supply, then the provider increases access to the available value added, even where the buyers are able to shop around for a lower value-for-money product. Constrained high value added supply increases the share of value added available to providers.

With high transaction cost there is limited ability for other providers to gain from segmentation of the market. The converse of this is that low transaction cost improves the ability of buyers to gain from high value-for-money providers. The finding here is that a reduction in transaction costs reinforces value-for-money advantage.

Figure 23 *Demand and supply curves, and value proposition map showing*

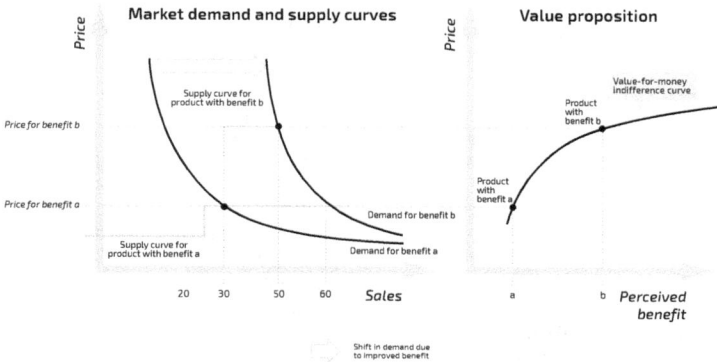

the impact of value-for-money advantage

Position 5 — Strategies based on shared transaction cost advantage

Transaction cost advantage is gained by removing shared transaction costs from parties wishing to transact directly with one another. In this strategy the platform reduces shared transaction costs, and as a consequence increases total value added available to platform users by this amount. In doing this the platform inserts itself in the value network with the opportunity to appropriate a share of the reduced transaction costs. Providers who choose not to use the platform are worse off because they offer poorer value-for-money compared to using the platform.

Platforms are extraordinary business opportunities where significant shared transaction costs are removed. Having said this, this transaction cost advantage is undermined where there is a general reduction in transaction cost that occurs independently of the platform.

MSPs crucially depend on cross-group effects being stimulated between the parties transacting on the platform. The strength of the cross-group effect increases, as the number of parties on the platform increases, and the bargaining power of the platform provider increases, but is always limited by the threats of disintermediation and multi-homing. Where increased usage is associated with declining cost economies or further reduction in shared transaction costs, then these feedback effects can further strengthen the bargaining power of the platform provider.

The implication for business strategy

High value-for-money advantage is robust in response to reductions in transaction cost. This conclusion also holds for cost advantage, which is a special case of value-for-money advantage where product quality is the same as that provided by others. Extemporaneous, local and transaction cost advantages are undermined by a general reduction in transaction cost. Business opportunities derived from value-for-money advantage, or reduction in transaction costs, do not change the focus of the opportunity on a particular place in a value network.

Costs that influence contractual relationships

Agency cost

Aside from buying and selling products, other reasons for establishing contractual relationships include overcoming constraints, acquiring options, income smoothing and placing risk with the party most willing to bear it. While there are many reasons for forming formal relationships, generally, it is because of the efficiencies that arise from arrangements that create incentives on the behaviour of the parties involved. Contractual relationships are used by businesses to improve coordination, by ensuring close alignment of the interests between buyer and their suppliers, and in this way better achieve their objectives. These relationships can be formal, for example, through employment contracts or contracts for service with external suppliers. Alternatively, products can be acquired through simple commercial or market transactions. The purchase of consumables from a retailer is an example of a simple market transaction. Acquisition cost covers the combined cost of buying or making the product, and the cost of administering the work – these are agency costs and cover tasks such as preparing the specifications, advertising, evaluating tenders, monitoring performance, and remedying poor performance.

Acquisition cost is minimised by ensuring an appropriate alignment between the way the business chooses to transact and the governance structure it puts in place to manage the transaction. The interests of the parties could conflict because of the possibility for opportunistic behaviour. If each party could always be relied upon not to seek advantage when the opportunity arises, and behave as committed, contracts would not be needed. The objective of the parties is to ensure as close an alignment of their interests to the counter-party as possible. There are a number of ways of aligning the interests of the parties. These include using incentives and sanctions, close monitoring and governance arrangements. Governance is the management accountability mechanism and structure appropriate to a particular business's knowhow, systems and processes, and organisational structure. Each of these methods imposes agency costs on the parties. Agency costs rise according to the extent of divergence between the interests of the parties. Each of the parties to the contract can impose costs on the other party. For example, a buyer who frequently makes changes to specifications on the agreed output imposes costs on the supplier, which can make it unviable for the supplier to continue with the contract. From the point of view of the principal of the contract, where there are substantial problems in monitoring and/or measuring the performance of suppliers, it may be more efficient to invest in the capability and manage it internally, rather than contracting it out.

Generally speaking, it is more efficient for a business to contract out than to perform the work internally, when: the buyer is able to monitor the performance of the external suppliers; the cost of measuring supplier performance is a small part of the acquisition cost; the cost of the risk of failure by the supplier to perform as expected is low; and low investment is required specifically for the transaction. On the other hand, market mechanisms do not function where, amongst other things: the transaction specific assets have no alternative uses; the type of transaction occurs rarely; and high uncertainty is involved in successful delivery of the output.

Contract specific investment

Contract specific investment is a measure of the ease with which resources required to fulfil a contract can be redeployed to other uses, without significant loss of value should the contract end – so, there is no opportunity cost in switching these resources. Contract specific investment occurs where, as a consequence of establishing the formal relationships, highly specialist skills are required that, on ending the relationships, cannot be redeployed to other projects. They also occur where the supplier needs to make significant investment of time or money to purchase and/or learn new systems that are specific to the contract. They also include costs from breaking contracts such as leases, delays, risks, and costs that would be incurred by the supplier in the event that the contract were terminated before the end of the contract period.

When the specificity of the investment in a specific transaction is low, the buyer is able to contract with many potential suppliers, and the market provides the best outcome. Market governance occurs when the identity of the parties to the transaction are unimportant, the nature of the agreement is carefully delimited, remedies for failure to perform are predictable, and third party participation is discouraged. As the specificity of the investment by the supplier in recurrent transactions increases, there are fewer potential suppliers who can undertake the transaction on acceptable terms and conditions. Bilateral governance occurs when the identity of the parties is as important as the relationship that has developed over time, and there is a presumption that it will continue in the future (if it did not the supplier would not invest in contract special assets). This will eventually result in a situation where the buyer owns, rather than contracts for, the asset on the open market. When a transaction is taken out of the market and is performed in-house by way of, say, an internal contracting system, it is unified governance.

From the buyer's point of view, the situation changes where transactions occur only occasionally. As the specificity of the investment in occasional transactions increases, the buyer is forced to move to appointing a third party arbitrator to determine aspects of the transaction that cannot be clearly specified upfront. Trilateral governance occurs when the contract cannot provide for all contingencies at the outset and, where contingencies are identified, the remedy is not known until some future point. Under trilateral governance structures a third party, such as an arbitrator, is often called upon to resolve disputes and to evaluate performance. In practice it is common to see a merging of aspects of these generic governance structures.

Uncertainty

Contracting parties often face uncertainty from unpredictable changes in circumstances. This problem is exacerbated where there are difficulties in clearly and unambiguously specifying the nature of the contract beforehand. Increasing the level of uncertainty does not alter the preferred governance relationships for non-specific transactions, since new commercial relationships are easily arranged.

Uncertainty poses problems where transaction specific investment is required. The buyer can address this by:

- standardising some of the features and simplifying the requirements so that more potential suppliers are available.
- withdrawing the need to provide high specificity assets and contracting for capability.
- maintaining the features but building more comprehensive governance arrangements, such as contractual provisions that require disputes to be referred to an independent expert or an arbitrator for resolution.

Where this is unworkable, the buyer can bring the transaction in-house, as part of the production process, using the internal organisational structure for governance.

There are two aspects of separating the capability to deliver from the ownership of assets in contracting decisions, the first is whether the asset is integral to the business's core competency and, second, whether asset ownership is an important factor to buyers in the contracting decision. The alternatives available are:

- Capacity is provided by the buyer. The asset is also owned by the buyer where it is integral to the business's core competency. Where this is not the case, assets can be acquired under an asset lease.
- Capacity is provided by the supplier. The buyer provides assets as a tactic to reduce dependence on the supplier, and reduces barriers to entry and exit of suppliers where it is cost ineffective for suppliers to invest in the asset. Aside from these cases the supplier also provides the assets, as, for example occurs under competitive market contracts.

Choosing between these alternatives will depend on the type of assets in question and the attendant costs and risks. The provision of non-specific assets could be owned by the buyer or supplier without any need for reversion of ownership at the end of the contract. For highly specific assets the range of answers is more complex.

Minimising acquisition costs

The decision tree in Figure 24 illustrates ways different conditions lead to different purchasing practice, risk sharing, contract type, quality assurance mechanisms, asset ownership and control, and governance arrangements. There are a range of possible governance arrangements. These include owning the resource to deliver the capacity internally, forming a joint venture, establishing a preferred supplier relationship, or simply negotiating a contract for supply with an independent party. The decision tree uses the following factors to show their influence on the costs and risks of contracting. Namely whether:

- the product can be clearly defined and specified at the outset. This may require separating capacity and asset ownership considerations;
- potential suppliers would be prepared to make the investment required to deliver the product;
- risk adjusted cost of failure to the buyer is high; and
- poor performance is easily identified and monitored and the cost of mitigants is in place.

There is scope to redesign products in ways for each of these factors, so that the cost of acquisition can be reduced to the buyer. The more successful the buyer is at this, the higher the likelihood that there is a competitive market available to deliver the product. In evaluating their alternatives a buyer will also consider their objectives and constraints. Figure 24 uses the example of acquiring input capacity. This analytical framework is at the nub of the assign method. Businesses operating the assign method develop knowhow, systems and processes in the formulation and management of appropriate relationships with the parties they transact with.

Figure 24 *Decision tree of some factors influencing the selection of a contractual relationship for acquiring input capacity*

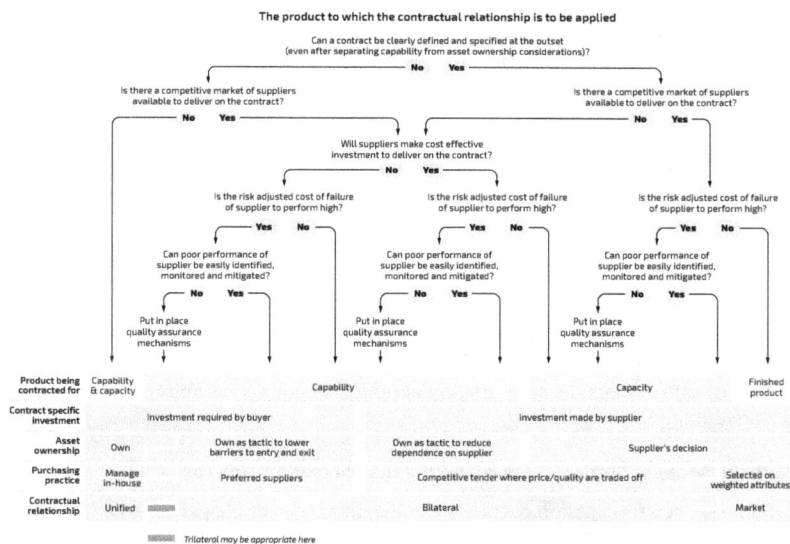

The product to which the contractual relationship is to be applied

Can a contract be clearly defined and specified at the outset
(even after separating capability from asset ownership considerations)?

Product being contracted for	Capability & capacity		Capability		Capacity	Finished product
Contract specific investment		Investment required by buyer			Investment made by supplier	
Asset ownership	Own	Own as tactic to lower barriers to entry and exit		Own as tactic to reduce dependence on supplier	Supplier's decision	
Purchasing practice	Manage in-house	Preferred suppliers		Competitive tender where price/quality are traded off		Selected on weighted attributes
Contractual relationship	Unified			Bilateral		Market

Trilateral may be appropriate here

Reduction in transaction costs and the reformation of the value network

Effects of reduction in transaction cost

From the point of view of the value network, five effects come into play when transaction costs are removed. These effects occur whether there is a market wide reduction or the reduction is brought about on a platform, in which case the impact is confined to the users of the platform. First, there is an increase in the range of products purchased as businesses move to buy in products rather than using in-house production. Second, this is accompanied by adjustment to activity type used by businesses. These effects occur in both buyers and suppliers. Third, competition increases, businesses with value-for-money advantage gain, and this is accompanied by the exit from the market of businesses pursuing extemporaneous, local and transaction cost advantages. Fourth, the value added of buyers improves and, finally, market demand increases.

The need to refine the business angle

Increase in the range of products purchased is accompanied by adjustment to activity type used by businesses. This is both in buyers and suppliers. The removal of transaction costs requires businesses to refine their activity type. Businesses focus on the opportunity at a particular place in the value network, and shed capabilities that are not core competencies through contractual relationships when responding to reductions in transaction costs. An impact of the reduction in transaction costs is that business angles are changed to accommodate more contracting for inputs.

For all market positioning strategies, reducing transaction costs increases total value added in a market. Reduction in transaction costs in a market increases demand for the product, the value added in the market, and value-for-money. Removing transaction costs also provides more opportunities for suppliers of products. One of the consequences of this is that more capabilities are outsourced. This applies in each of the element markets in which a business operates.

Businesses respond to this situation by:

- Reviewing their capabilities to identify those that are core competencies and those that do not have strong case for being a core competency.
- Selecting an activity type appropriate for the business without these capabilities.
- Given that other businesses in the market are also doing this, refining the business opportunity to reflect the emerging market context.
- Refining the activity type to create a new business angle.

Businesses with value-for-money advantage gain, and this is accompanied by the loss of sales by businesses pursuing extemporaneous, local and transaction cost advantages.

Business opportunities from removing shared transaction cost

Some shared transaction costs are significant to one, or all, parties to a transaction. Solutions that remove a set of dominant shared transaction costs faced by large groups of users, built using highly scalable systems and processes, are platforms. The types of shared transaction costs solved are: information discovery problems between buyers and suppliers, and senders and receivers, which facilitate exchange in receiving and accepting offers; and the problem of lemons, where a buyer does not know in advance the quality of the product they are buying, and facilitates payment transfers by the trustworthy settlement of sales between buyers and suppliers, and senders and receivers for transfer payments. These are single-sided market opportunities focused on providing a solution to reduce dominant sources of transaction cost.

These platforms can be specific for one market sector, and there can be opportunities for many different sets of shared transaction costs to be removed from the one market sector – creating MSP+s. In the sector there could be platforms that focus on providing directories. Hotels are an example, where others provide reviews, and there are separate opportunities for others to provide facilities to book and pay for a hotel. In addition there are opportunities to provide the payment facilities, such as credit cards and digital wallets, so that hotel rooms and restaurants can be paid for.

The benefits to parties transacting with one another, from removing shared transaction costs, can be so significant that in some settings they can give rise to a new business opportunity for a multi-sided platform. Where these are disruptive to the market and costs of transacting over platforms become negligible, then it becomes feasible to transact low price items over platforms. Using the travel industry once again, platforms now list spare bedrooms in people's homes. For the provider of accommodation, the cost of offering and transacting on a platform, provisioning the accommodation and any inconvenience, is now less than the income from providing the accommodation.

As transaction costs are removed from a value network it matures, and barriers to transacting on the platforms provide new opportunities for businesses to participate on the platform as providers of exchange and applications products – mail houses that print invoices and statements on behalf of large senders are an example in the postal platform. On internet platforms, these are referred to as enabling the building of an ecosystem of other support suppliers, such as developers of plugins and themes.

With the development of information and technology systems, and the knowhow to provide highly scalable solutions to the information: discovery, information exchange, the problem of lemons, and payments, there are also opportunities to provide infrastructure to support platforms for others to apply. These solutions in turn can be supported by an ecosystem of support suppliers.

Summary

Reduction in transaction costs is devastating for businesses pursuing extemporaneous, local and transaction cost advantage market positioning strategies. Value-for-money advantage is robust in the face of reductions in transaction costs. A consequence of a reduction in transaction costs in a market is an increase in the opportunities to establish contractual supply arrangements with providers, and through this to reform the activity type. Allied, and a counterweight to this, are new opportunities to provide products under contract. In responding to reductions in transaction costs, businesses focus on the opportunity at a particular place in the value network, and shed capabilities that are not core competencies, through contractual relationships. This entails businesses to reconfigure their activity type around their core competencies.

This requires greater use of contracting, and it is in the interests of the buyer to ensure suppliers are closely aligned to the buyer's interests. There are a number of ways to do this, including the use of incentives and sanctions, close monitoring and formal contracts. Each of these methods imposes costs on the buyer and suppliers. These transaction costs rise as the business intentions of the two parties diverge. There are four conditions where it is more efficient for a buyer to contract out, and buy a product in the market, than to perform the work internally. First, where no significant difficulties exist in monitoring the performance of agents (suppliers or distributors for example). Second, where the cost of measuring performance is minor. Third, where the risk of failure is low and would not undermine the ongoing survival of the buyer. Fourth, where the specificity of the capability required is low. Where these four conditions apply, conditions are conducive to external supply of products. Where these conditions do not exist, then a hybrid form of relationship may be more appropriate, or even, having the capability in-house.

Transaction costs create business opportunities in:

- Contracted supply of inputs.
- Single-sided platforms focused on providing a solution to reduce dominant sources of transaction cost.
- MSP+ in settings where significant reduction in shared transaction costs are coupled with strong cross-group effects exist between the user groups.
- Exchange and applications products on platforms.
- Provision of infrastructure to support platforms.

Selected literature review

Early origin of idea

An early description of the impact of friction on different economic factors was given in 1758 by François Quesnay in *Tableau Économique*. The type of friction he referred to is regulation.

Key influences on the work

The leading work on transaction costs in determining the boundary of the business is explored by Oliver Williamson. See for example the papers 'Transaction-Cost Economics: The Governance of Contractual Relations' in a 1979 edition of *Journal of Law and Economics*; and 'Strategizing, Economizing, and Economic Organisation' in *Strategic Management* published in 1991. Also see the paper by Grossman and Hart in a 1986 edition of the *Journal of Political Economy* titled 'The costs and benefits of ownership: A theory of vertical and lateral integration'.

An early application of cooperative game theory to business strategy is the paper by Brandenburger and Stuart 'Value-based Business Strategy' published in a 1996 edition of the *Journal of Economics and Management Strategy*.

EIGHT
Turbulent markets are gold rushes so travel light with only essential core competencies

During the 1980s and 1990s there were major changes in the pattern of ownership of the largest commercial forests in the USA. In 1996 14.6 million hectares were owned by the largest 11 forest owners. Of these, two were not involved in processing, with the remaining nine owners being publicly listed, vertically integrated, wood product processors. Twenty years prior to this, all of the largest commercial forest owners were vertically integrated corporations. In the period 1976 to 1996 four of these corporations made no change to the ownership structure of their forests during the period, while five utilised a variety of structures that brought about changes in forest ownership. One placed some of its forests into a limited partnership, only to later terminate it and consolidate the forests back into the public corporation. In 1998 two processing businesses sold forests, each of more than 28,000 hectares, to private investors. A year later six more deals, each of more than 36,000 hectares were on the market. Such sales typically involve putting in place a supply contract back to the wood processor.

Congruent with these changes, large pension funds and fund managers have invested directly in forestry as part of building diversified portfolios. Such investments with long-term horizons match their membership obligations and investment styles. Over the period 1981 to 1997 funds under management and invested in forests increased from US$100 million in 1981, to US$2.0 billion in 1992, to US$5.6 billion in 1997. By 1997 these funds represented some 10 percent of the market value of privately owned commercial forests. These new owners have, as a general rule, adopted business models where all forestry services are purchased in on-contract from specialist suppliers when required – so they have low overhead costs with most costs variable.

Introduction

Market turbulence changes the nature of the market context faced by the business. Market turbulence comes in many forms, for example from changes in buyer tastes, innovation, competition, asset bubbles, and economic conditions such as recession. Market turbulence is a fact of commerce. Some businesses are able to respond to market turbulence better than others because they have capabilities to speculate, or have invested in the capacity to respond to change.

Turbulent markets also offer new business opportunities, some of which attract new entrants.

This chapter discusses the impact of market instability on business angles and the choice of activity type. The case is made that during times of market turbulence businesses develop business angles using the activity type that requires least ownership of assets, investing only in essential core competencies and contracting for other capabilities. During times of market turbulence it is difficult for businesspeople to gauge whether they can profit from a perceived business opportunity. The remainder of the chapter is structured into two sections. The next section discusses the drivers of market turbulence and how market turbulence increases uncertainty. This is followed by a discussion of how high uncertainty drives the choice to business angles that simplify the core resources and reduce the need for the investment of own capital. The key determinants of the range of viable alternative activity types are the expected proportion of return from speculation and the rate of market growth. Expectations of a high proportion of return from speculation and rate of market growth, are associated with a wider range of activity types being used to formulate business angles to share in the expected value added.

Market turbulence

Mega-trends

Markets are always in a state of flux, although the rate of change may not always be visible to those involved, because they are immersed in the change. Changes in the market are made visible by monitoring alterations in the constituents of the value network, specifically the relative market share of all players at each stage in a value network, and changes in the shape and participants in value network over time. These changes can be quite pronounced over even a few years.

An example to show the nature of these alterations comes from the forestry sector in New Zealand, where over the period 1992 to 2002 there was a significant growth in investment in commercial small-scale forests. In 1992 the investment in small-scale forests (of less than 1,000 ha) was dominated by farmers and other landowners in forestry, for erosion control and windbreaks, and as a crop on marginal farmland. Tree species with timber of commercial value were frequently planted. There were also a small number of commercial forestry companies, some of which were also engaged in producing poles and posts for sale. By 1998 the make-up of market share by stage in the value network had changed dramatically with the growth of investment in new greenfield small-scale forests. Much of this growth was supplied by promoters, who responded to a demand for investment in small-scale forests by creating special purpose investment vehicles for the planting and management of new forests. Shares in these investment vehicles where then sold to private investors. Some forestry consultants also promoted investments of this type. These ventures did not always own land, but entered into agreements with landowners for the use of their land in return for shares in the venture. The changes in the value network over this ten year time period are depicted in Figure 25. The mega-trend evident over the second part of this time period was a continuous fall in log prices. The corresponding fall in expected returns from investment in forestry put an end to the demand for investment in small-scale forests.

There are three observations here. As a result of these changes new businesses entered into the market. This is an example of businesses developing business angles with an expectation of developing core competencies, and with risk/return/capital characteristics attractive to investors with different preferences. The value network becomes fragmented with the emergence of new stages in the value network. Value networks change over time as they respond and transform in response to mega-trends. Mega-trends present business opportunities. Expectations of trends in prices, and the ongoing search for an angle on a business opportunity, means that where appropriate conditions exist, the observed market behaviour is bouts of spontaneous market instability, as new businesses come into a market. New entrants utilise a range of different activity types to create business angles, in order to participate in the market and to attract investment. The business angles put to market are determined by the nature of the demand for investment with specific characteristics (size of investment and risk/return conditions under which it is made available), activity types that are feasible, and the nature of the perceived business opportunity.

Figure 25 *Value network maps of market share and key participants producing investment products in small-scale forestry in New Zealand in 1992, 1998 and 2002*

**Stages in the value network producing products
for investment in small-scale forestry**

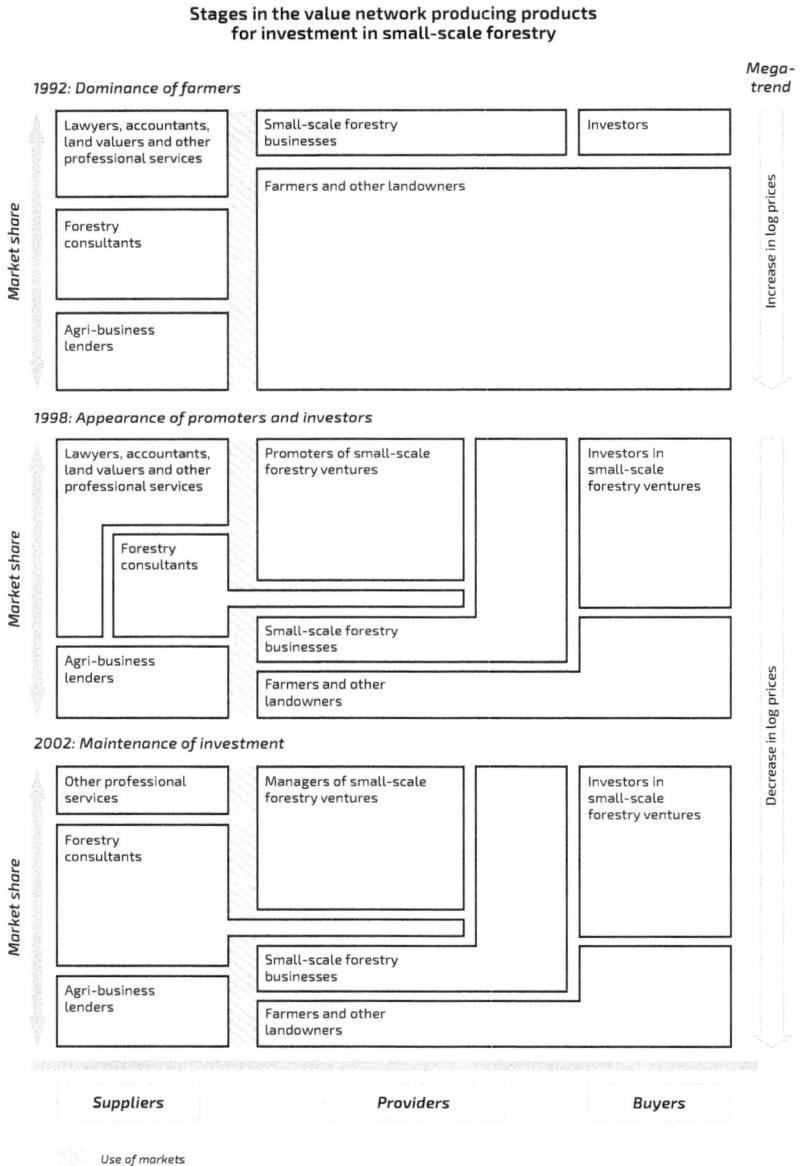

1992: Dominance of farmers

Mega-trend

Market share

| Lawyers, accountants, land valuers and other professional services | Small-scale forestry businesses | Investors |

Farmers and other landowners

Forestry consultants

Agri-business lenders

Increase in log prices

1998: Appearance of promoters and investors

Market share

| Lawyers, accountants, land valuers and other professional services | Promoters of small-scale forestry ventures | Investors in small-scale forestry ventures |

Forestry consultants

Small-scale forestry businesses

Agri-business lenders

Farmers and other landowners

Decrease in log prices

2002: Maintenance of investment

Market share

| Other professional services | Managers of small-scale forestry ventures | Investors in small-scale forestry ventures |

Forestry consultants

Small-scale forestry businesses

Agri-business lenders

Farmers and other landowners

| **Suppliers** | **Providers** | **Buyers** |

Use of markets

Trajectory of value networks

The trajectory followed by markets is the path traced by successive plays by businesses to gain a share of the expected value added. Value added is captured by creating a new market with a supporting cluster, which forms a value network. It can also be captured by causing a favourable reallocation of value added in an existing value network by creating a new clustering of participants. A favourable reallocation of value added can also take place between the parties of an existing cluster. Any and each of the five element markets in which the business operates is a place where change can be initiated.

Once in motion, markets under rapid and enduring change quickly lose the legacy of the old. Markets do not necessarily follow trajectories of continuous refreshing of products, with each successive refresh providing improved product benefits. At times, through the intervention of high value-for-money alternatives, the trajectory is redirected along a new path. The introduction of online auction sites profoundly changing the market for classified advertising in newspapers by virtually extinguishing demand, is an illustration of this. The forces that cause punctuated market trajectories are different from those driving the evolution of objects. Forces that drive the evolution of objects are adaptation to purpose, technology, fashion and economic conditions. Objects such as chairs and tables, even when they are in widespread use, have precedents, whereas the value networks associated with the delivery of the objects can change unrecognisably over time. One drive for businesses to do this is to increase the value of a business's resources. This objective gives priority to those resources best able to achieve this. Another driver is to take advantage of uncertainty in markets and to speculate that an initiative will deliver expected positive results. The outcome of speculation can take a business along any of the development paths, and may even compromise its lifecycle.

Market volatility produces uncertainty

Turning now to the speculation driver, during times of high market turbulence value networks are in change and are being reformed into new configurations. This is through changes to the network composition as a result of consolidation and rationalisation of the participants, and through capital flows in the form of investment, divestment, closures and the growth/loss in the quantum of value added available. During such upheavals there is a wide variety of business opportunities for businesses, and these businesses utilise a range of quite different activity types to construct business angles. Despite the abundance of perceived opportunities, high market turbulence is associated with high uncertainty. This is because businesspeople operating in turbulent markets find it difficult to form a generally accepted view on the emerging direction. Market volatility produces uncertainty in a market that makes it difficult to discriminate between potential winners and losers. The absence of clear favourites, in turn, provides the conditions for the formulation of new opportunities and business angles.

This presents a complex set of dynamics. In markets with continued high uncertainty due to market turbulence, two effects come into operation. First, for incumbents, investment falls off because of high uncertainty and the difficulty in picking which of these participants is most likely to succeed. These businesses respond by focusing on essential core resources and the business becomes simpler, in the sense of managing fewer capabilities. They focus on economising

- namely, minimising their need for purchasing resources by entering into supply arrangements with resource owners. In some circumstances this rationalisation can lead to increased concentration in the sector through mergers and acquisitions. Second, those parts of the value network, where there are perceived profit opportunities, also become attractive to new entrants to develop business angles using a range of quite different activity types. Investment in new entrants increases. New entrants obtain resources and investment by entering into supply arrangements with resource owners. These resources and investment are sourced from parties most ready to bear the risk for the expected return.

These two effects positively reinforce one another, with incumbents consolidating those parts of the value network that offer better returns on existing core competencies, and new entrants focusing on those parts of the value network where existing core competencies provide little or no advantage. The greater the perceived profit opportunity, then the more new entrants who participate, which in turn attracts more investment. As long as volatility continues, new entrants come into the market willing to take a hand at the speculator's table. In short, volatility opens market opportunities to new entrants. New entrants start with minimum resourcing, prioritised to create essential core competencies. Established businesses that face market volatility respond by reducing the scope of the business angle to encompass only valuable existing core competencies. This is done by transforming the activity type, and exploring the development paths to improve the value for the resources the business possesses.

Volatile markets and returns from speculation

At its core, market volatility is a pricing issue, and occurs in all markets in which a business operates. Price volatility permeates between markets. This is clearly seen in the relationship between business profitability, its market value and the value of resources that are made scarce. But this is not a simple relationship where the price of resources, and the business, flow from the ability to capture value in the form of profit. Resources can have their own demand and supply dynamics, which set their price. This, for example, is evident in farm land prices that fluctuate in ways quite unrelated to its expected productive value in farming, and farm produce prices. A value network can develop consisting of parties seeking to share in the flow of money associated with speculation in farm land, and this is not the same as the flow of money associated with farming.

A number of value networks can converge in a market. Market volatility transmits through markets via prices. Each market has its own set of demand considerations for a resource, which contributes to its overall demand. Where a market appears in many value networks, each value network presents an opportunity for its use to be switched from one value network to another, according to the pricing in each market.

Market instability and barriers to entry

Barriers to entry, including high transaction costs and institutional arrangements, can inhibit businesses from responding to market turbulence, as they impose constraints on reconfiguring the business so as to increase their value, and accessing buyers and suppliers in each of the markets in which the business operates. The choice of activity type is one way to overcome barriers to entry. Attributes of an activity type are favourable for entering a market when they result in four conditions being met. First, the cost difference between incumbents and new entrant is low so that the accumulation of past experience and other economies creates little in the way of barriers to entry. Second, there are no, or weak, supply-side positive feedback effects, for example, from returns to scale. And, third, there are constraints on capacity that limit the maximum output of businesses. The fourth additional requirement is that scarce resources controlled by incumbents do not inhibit entry. Where these conditions are satisfied, the response to market turbulence is new entrants entering the market. Where these conditions are not satisfied, then incumbents can consolidate and dominate the industry.

Response to volatile markets

Potential new business angles

Volatile markets present opportunities in all five orders of market play, including their combinations. As described in chapter 5, operating several orders of market play is integral to some business angles. The breadth of opportunities can be gauged by bearing in mind that each of the five contributors to value (as described in chapter 2) can be applied to the five orders of market play. Businesses potentially can develop core competencies in each of these orders. High perceived opportunities for profit results in a larger number of new participants vying to insert themselves in a market. This motion in a market has consequences for the other participants in a value network, and can result in changing the shape of the value network.

Working to produce products within the value network for a final consumer (Order 1 market play) presents the most widely recognised business angles for improvement and refinements. Businesses continually strive to make improvements to maintain and improve their competitive position. New entrants also need to quickly emulate these levels of competitive performance, and improve profitability. Being able to attain these levels of competitive performance comes from the five contributors to value. For example:

- **Contributor 1** Striving to offer better value-for-money than alternatives covers initiatives that focus on product design and the customer experience provided, as well as re-positioning in the value network.
- **Contributor 2** Increasing productivity through the selection and purchasing of inputs.
- **Contributor 3** Refining the business angle and organisational structure to better exploit the perceived opportunity, and continuously improving the productivity of the production process.
- **Contributor 4** Improving the reliability to deliver on business plans by use of risk mitigants, and the resilience of on-going profitability through the use of strategic options.
- **Contributor 5** Enhancing the FCF value of the business through use of financial markets. This extends to disposal of poor performing assets and use of capital gearing.

High volatility drives new entrants to use business angles with only essential core competencies, minimal capital and risk allocated to the party most willing to bear it

Uncertainty is created in a market when there is change in any of the following: market growth rate (which is positive in growing markets or negative in declining markets); the share of value added captured by a business; expectations over the length of time this continues and the rate of change in the redistribution of value added between participants in the value network. Market volatility is a normal part of business and its impact on profit is also dictated by change in value-for-money of alternatives, including those due to competitive actions. The duration of the volatile period is constrained by the strength of barriers to entry; regulatory and institutional arrangements (including monopolistic market positions); and feedback effects in multi-sided markets. Businesspeople can respond to this high uncertainty by choosing business angles using activity types with only essential core competencies requiring least owned assets. In this way, they can minimise the capital requirements and allocate risk to the party most willing to bear it.

From business opportunity to business angle

The existence of this wide range of quite different activity types reflects the result of a process of entrepreneurial discovery in which an angle on a perceived business opportunity is identified for pursuit. Taking an illustration, direct investors in forests are speculating there will be a market for their logs and that they will have the appropriate resources of land, labour and capital to deliver logs to market profitably – businesses undertaking this activity are classified as utilising the *assemble-assemble* activity. Investors in other activities associated with this investment may also seek to share in the profit generated by growing forests to produce logs, but without incurring the same capital requirements and commercial risk as direct investment in a self-contained forestry business. This is done by investing in a business that owns only trees and land, with non-forest resources being provided by assignment to the work. Forestry businesses undertaking this activity are classified as utilising the *assemble-assignment* activity.

Turbulent markets are also associated with a high proportion of planned profit being contributed by speculation. With high asset price speculation there will more investment in these assets than at other times, as the FCF value calculation includes expected increase in asset values as income. Returning to the example of the forestry business owning land and trees, with high asset speculation in farm land the forestry business might plan to convert the land to farm land after logging. The income from land conversion may be an important component of the profitability of the forestry investment.

An implication of placing the business opportunity perceived by businesspeople at the centre of the analysis, is that it exposes businesspeople to the reality of the impossibility of predicting the future, and the impact of unforeseen situations on the final outcome of an investment. Once having made the decision to invest, businesspeople continually seek to parlay this position. In this way businesses are constantly building on their current position with the aim of magnifying and extending its life. Businesspeople play for some unknown and unknowable return on the applied resources. One of the ramifications of the fact that there is a range of different activity types, is that for any perceived business opportunity there, consequently, is a range of angles through which to exploit that opportunity.

Summary

Opportunities arise in turbulent markets: because value networks are reshaped as new places in the value network open up; and because it generates uncertainty about which incumbents will survive, which in turn opens up opportunities for speculation. The greater the market volatility and market size, the greater the value of the business opportunities from new business angles and speculation. Because of this, businesses that seek to disrupt a market do not have it all to themselves. Far from being a 'king hit' knocking competitors out of a market, a market disruption play can herald an arms race between competitors.

For businesses seeking opportunities to take advantage of market turbulence, the rate of market turbulence changes the business angle by simplifying the core resources, and by allocating risk to parties willing to assume it. To do this, use is made of activity types that use the assign method to deliver outputs and to acquire inputs. Having said this, profitability is brought back into the market by some businesses developing activity types that create scarce resources, which might include the removal of transaction costs through horizontal integration of the value network.

Selected literature review

Early origin of idea

The study of the structure of industries has a long history dating back to Adam Smith's 1776 ground-breaking book *An Inquiry into the Nature and Causes of the Wealth of Nations*.

Key influences on the work

Market structure is now a well-studied topic and it is of interest to competition regulation bodies. An example of this work is 'The Evolution of New Industries and the Determinants of Market Structure' by Klepper and Graddy published in a 1990 edition of *The RAND Journal of Economics*. An exploration of the impact of random influences and positive feedback effects on industry concentration is given in Ormerod's 1994 book *Butterfly Economics* published by Faber and Faber Limited.

The dynamic capability funded by the option premium is discussed by Teece in the 2007 paper 'Explicating dynamic capabilities: the nature and microfoundations of (sustainable) enterprise performance' published in the *Strategic Management Journal*.

NINE
Business opportunities have an unpredictable lifecycle so mind the options

The auditing, accounting and advisory business KPMG was formed by a series of mergers on both sides of the Atlantic. The roots of these mergers go back to accounting businesses established in London (1870), Glasgow (1877), Amsterdam (1917), and New York (1925). By the late 1980s KPMG was one of the 'big eight' business advisory businesses providing accounting, auditing, tax and management consulting services from offices around the world. Legal services were then added in some jurisdictions. This growth by merger and diversification was a common feature with all but one of the big eight. Mergers continued and by 1998 KPMG was one of the big five.

This growth has not been without cost. A significant cost to the partners is the risk of litigation on the outcome of advice and guidance given. This cost is mitigated through investment in training, internal risk mitigating knowhow, systems and processes, and insurance. The collapse of the US public corporation Enron Corporation in 2001, audited by Arthur Anderson, had repercussions for the, by then, big five. The passing of the Sarbanes-Oxley Act (2002) in the US, in response to the Enron collapse, and subsequent changes to US stock exchange regulations, placed restrictions on public auditing businesses from providing non-auditing services to their audit clients. It was now the big four – Arthur Anderson was a direct casualty of the Enron failure.

KPMG responded by divesting its consulting and legal operations. The most significant of these divestitures was the listing of its consulting and technology arm on the New York Stock Exchange in 2001, as BearingPoint Inc. In 2009 the business's US operation filed for Chapter 11 bankruptcy. BearingPoint continues today as a partnership in Europe. KPMG continues as a successful auditing, accounting and advisory business.

Introduction

The lifecycle of most businesses parallels the energy and commitment given to them by the founder owner. The lifecycle of these businesses mirrors the working life of the founder owner, but is cut short by the demise of its market. A market opportunity has a lifecycle unrelated to a business's ownership decisions. Choice of activity type provides a way to match the objectives, constraints and planned lifespan of a business, with the nature of the business opportunity, its expected lifecycle and market context.

This chapter discusses the consequences of uncertainty in the lifespan of a business angle on its value. Following this introduction, the forces that determine the lifespan of a business angle are outlined. The relationship between the lifespan of a business angle and uncertainty are then explored. The roles of activity type are then outlined.

Coinsidence of lifecycles and lifespans

The life expectancy of a business

At any point in time the owners of a business can determine when to cease trading and liquidate its assets. Numerically most businesses are liquidated, but businesses with valuable resources can merge, acquire other businesses, be acquired, or divest their assets. While the lifecycle of a business can parallel and embody a business opportunity, this is not a direct relationship. For example, for businesses with multiple product lines, each pursuing separate opportunities in different markets, they may be relatively immune to the loss of any one opportunity. Extrapolating this, the business opportunity itself could be to operate a portfolio of investments in a range of quite different business angles.

The lifespan of a business angle is determined by its purpose. The life expectancy of a venture can be designed to have a fixed term, or to be terminated on the attainment of an event. For example, many ventures in the film industry operate in this manner. Alternatively the expectation is that the business has continuity over time, generating on-going profits. While the purpose may define the planned life of the venture, the actual lifecycle of the business opportunity is determined by market context. Change, particularly significant unanticipated change, can herald the end of an opportunity for a business; and for the business itself where the business is unable to parlay its position into a new opportunity. Market conditions can become unfavourable suddenly and without warning, for instance where the major buyer of a supplier is put into receivership owing their suppliers money. Suppliers caught unaware and unable to recover owed money can also collapse.

Not only are markets in change, the parties to a value network cluster can be swapped in and out, based on the value-for-money they contribute, precipitated for example through entry of new participants and the exit of incumbents.

The presence of positive feedback effects can make a business particularly susceptible to the impact of unfavourable changes in competitive conditions and market context where they operate on the drivers of positive feedback. MSP+s are a class of businesses that are vulnerable to changes in market context that undermine the strength of its value proposition to users. With sufficient loss in the value proposition to users positive cross-group effects are quickly lost. Where positive feedback effects operate, the life expectancy of a business angle can change rapidly in both the rate it grows, and the rate at which it collapses.

Spontaneous industries

Some businesses are specifically established to take advantage of a particular set of circumstances. Spontaneous industries are short-lived clusters of businesses in a locality centred on a single industry. These clusters emerge where conditions are conducive and last for only as long as those conditions persist. These conditions are idiosyncratic, related to specific institutional conditions, natural resources, talents and opportunities faced by one or a few individuals in a location. They gain little benefit by way of economies derived from clustering with other businesses in that geographic location. As a consequence these businesses can be part of long value networks, for example involving long supply chains, and as a consequence are vulnerable to forces which reform the value network.

In addition, businesses established at short lead-time to take advantage of speculative opportunities can have lifespans that are difficult to estimate. The lifecycle of spontaneous industries and highly speculative ventures can be encapsulated in the phrase 'here-today-gone-tomorrow'.

Lifecycle of business opportunities

Studies of the evolution of industries over time show a three stage lifecycle. The early stage of an industry's lifecycle is characterised by market share instability, when there are many participants. Market share is stable and concentrated in the mature stage of the lifecycle. What happens mid-lifecycle can vary from an initial increase in the number of participants, before the reduction starts in the mature stage of the lifecycle, to a gradual reduction in the number of participants over the entire lifecycle.

From the viewpoint of the business, there are three stages in a business's exploitation of an opportunity over its lifecycle: start-up of a new entrant when the business tries to establish its place in a value network; on-going operation where a business seeks to maximise its value from the value network; and when a business is in stress and focused on maintaining profitability, for example because the business angle is coming to the end of its lifecycle. Nonetheless, the life expectancy of a business can be less than that of the opportunity because of business failure, or the same, or longer, by parlaying the initial position into new business angles. To varying degrees, businesses have to manage through three distinct situations:

- forging a place in a value network by adapting to market conditions and by refining the opportunity, business angle and business model with the aim of creating core competencies. For this the drive is to uncover knowledge about the business angle to prove and entrench the profitability of the business;

- maximising the capture of value added from the value network in the face of changes in competitive conditions and market contexts. Businesses at this stage of their lifecycle frequently also parlay their resources into new opportunities; and

- maintaining profitability from a value network undergoing structural change, such as those imposed by the introduction of a market disrupting product. For this the capacity to respond to new trajectories over the remaining life of the business opportunity is the challenge because markets do not necessarily follow trajectories for which past experience is relevant.

The relationship between a business angle's lifespan and uncertainty

Aligning the business to the business opportunity lifecycle

Recall that FCF value of a business is the net present value of expected profits over its lifetime and that the uncertainty premium is the cost to ensure that plans are met and the option premium is the cost to ensure the on-going continuity of the business. Businesses have different objectives as to their lifetime, and consequently strategic options have differing degrees of relevance in decision making to each business. Overlying this objective, the competitive conditions and market context faced by a business can change dramatically over time. This can make calculation of FCF value difficult because of uncertainty about the lifespan and trajectory of the business angle. In these situations businesses choose different levels of expenditure on a portfolio of salient strategic options according to the conditions facing the business at the time.

A high capacity to respond to uncertainty, with the capability to generate scarce resources, creates sustainable competitive advantage because the business is able to respond and gain from conditions as they emerge in the market. These businesses are primed to take advantage of serendipity - at least in the domain of some of the contributors to value. Having the capacity to respond to uncertainty, but possessing no capacity to make scarce resources, simply confines the business to survival, earning no profit - or even worse, becoming the 'walking dead' where it is less costly for the business to continue trading than to close. This can occur where there are contractual costs that the owner may still have to pay after the termination of the business, for example the remaining term of leases on premises, plant and equipment.

A high capability to create scarce resources, with low capacity to respond to uncertainty, will not make the cut in the market, and this trajectory leads to the demise of these scarce resources. It is also difficult to envisage a future for businesses with a low capacity to respond to uncertainty, and no capacity to generate scarce resources. These conditions are most often seen in businesses that have systematically under-invested in maintaining the income earning capacity of their capabilities. Formerly well-managed businesses can end up in this position under the leadership of managers who mistakenly confuse accounting profit for measures of the existence of scarce resources within the business. It is for this reason 'buyer beware' when acquiring distressed businesses. A business turnaround manager can restore the accounting profitability of a failing venture for a while by removing costs, and in doing so destroy its core competencies. This is a sobering example of confusing accounting profit for a measure of the payments received from scarce resources, which it is not.

Sources of uncertainty addressed by the uncertainty premium

It is important to clearly distinguish the uncertainty associated with meeting business plans and budgets from the uncertainty over the continuity of the business. Uncertainty refers to the degree to which plans, and underpinning information, are unable to adequately prepare a business for the actual events that occur. These events apply to all contributors to business value covered in its plans and budgets. For example:

- **Price uncertainty** exists in the markets a business operates in. This is due to ambiguity about the strength of the business's bargaining power, customer needs and the alternatives they face, and competitor considerations. Through the price quantity demand relationship, price uncertainty translates into uncertainty about sales and revenue levels. Price uncertainty also applied to inputs.

- **Opportunity uncertainty** concerns the actual sales opportunities, the timing and ability to collect the cash owed to the business, and emerging changes in market demand.

- **Input uncertainty** relates to the type, specification, mix, terms and conditions of the availability of inputs.

- **Capability uncertainty** refers to the ability of businesses to execute plans. It covers considerations that impact on a business's productivity, such as, of the state of knowledge and technology, managerial behaviours (for example, risk aversion), the response of internal stakeholders (for example, power struggles and poor ability to execute), and the ability to accept change (for example, the acceptability of change to the norms of the organisation).

- **Decision uncertainty** covers the awareness and interpretation of change: the formulation of responses and their timing; action interdependencies; knowledge of direct, indirect and unintended consequences; and the ability to respond to mistakes and adverse circumstances. Decision uncertainty stands distinct from uncertainty about future business opportunities and availability of inputs.

- **Regulatory and institutional uncertainty** is due to ambiguity and inconsistency in the legal, regulatory and institutional environment that impact on commercial contracts and contractual relationships.

- **Business value uncertainty** is wide ranging and relates to matters as diverse as changes to legal structures, and timing of any sale or wind up of the assets of the business.

The uncertainty premium recognises the costs incurred from these sources and the costs to mitigate them in order to meet plans and budgets. The choice of position in the value network and activity type, is used to put in place an appropriate capital, risk and return profile. Investing resources in knowhow, systems and processes also mitigates risk; as can the choice of appropriate business strategy, organisational architecture, incentive schemes and the acquisition of new knowledge. Arrangements to pass risk, at a price, to parties willing to bear it, are widely used. Such arrangements include the use of insurance, outsourcing contracts and tactical options, for example, the use of foreign currency contracts by exporters and importers.

Aligning strategic options to planned capacity

Having said this, failure to manage the uncertainty to realise business plans and budgets can jeopardise the continuity of the business. The consequence of business decisions to use resources to address an expected uncertain event is summarised as:

The planned for profit is the outturn of actual events; modified by planned actions to respond to planned for events; modified in turn by, available strategic options should the planned actions be insufficient.

This is a causative view where options provide the mechanism to recover from a sequence of events and responses, as well as to bring about something positive from the situation. The way to understand this mechanism is that the final state of a business decision to cope with an expected uncertain event is determined by the net result of a trigger event and actions to respond to it (including risk mitigation actions) modified by any effective capacity to respond.

Strategic options can mitigate the negative impact of adverse events. However, this can be insufficient to prevent the failure of a business, for example, in a market downturn, collapse, or structural change in the value network. The options put in place can be insufficient to deal with the circumstances that actually emerge. Options also provide the capacity to benefit from an event.

Organisational structure is not well suited to providing the capacity to respond

Despite a presumption that businesses make appropriate decisions and have capabilities able to respond well to change, this is frequently not the case, because when significant change does take place businesses can be slow to respond, and the response can be unstructured and ill-coordinated. The reason for this is that it is the organisational structure that determines a business's response to changes in market context. Organisational structure is not well suited to providing actions to ensure the continuity of the business.

The fundamental components of organisational structure are business strategy, organisational architecture, incentive schemes, and ways to acquire new knowledge. Organisational architecture relates to the assignment of decision-making rights, that is to say, the right to decide and to take action. The incentive schemes cover the performance evaluation, response and reward systems. These various components act on the expected profit from planned actions because of opportunities seized and mistakes avoided. Failure to realise planned profit is attributed to cost of opportunities missed and mistakes made by the business.

The ability to mitigate the cost of missed opportunities and mistakes is related to the nature of uncertainty the business faces. Uncertainty ranges from risk (that is, the known unknowns in which the likelihood of events occurring can be assessed); through to acknowledgement of unknown knowns, for example, severe rare events where the potential for occurrence is recognised even though their timing and impact may be unknown; and on through to an unknowable future.

Organisational architecture and incentives are used to reduce the cost stemming from likely mistakes, and the cost of mistakes, that arise from identifiable, significant, rare events. Reducing the cost of mistakes through organisational architecture and incentives is made at a trade-off of increased cost from the impact of unknowable unknowns. One reason for this is that the rigidity of organisational architecture, and incentives employed to address the specified risk, makes the business less able to respond to the unknowable.

Business strategy is used to reduce the cost of missing opportunities that are likely but rare events. Once again this is as a trade-off of the increased cost of the impact of the unknowable unknowns. The narratives provided by business strategy, supported by incentives that make it successful for dealing with likely rare events, make it difficult for organisations to respond to the unknowable future events. A reason for this is that institutionalised strategic planning functions are too far removed from the pulse of the market. While some businesses undertake R&D to acquire new knowledge, with the aim of pushing back the veil of uncertainty, frequently, organisations find it difficult to internalise this knowledge in the face of organisational structures with strong capabilities to deal with the cost of mistakes.

Business strategy, organisational architecture and incentives can have a profound impact on reducing the costs owing to mistakes and missed opportunity because of the application of knowhow, systems and processes. Better knowledge increases the range of strategic options.

In this setting, the cost of uncertainty is the sum of the costs owing to poor information and the costs owing to mistakes. When the degree of uncertainty is low, the source of risk faced by the business is dominated by the risk of mistakes. Where there are high levels of uncertainty, then the risk faced by the business increases significantly and the cost owing to missed opportunities becomes a significant source of risk.

The impact of uncertainty on the business will depend on the sum of impacts that includes those from likely, unknown and unknowable factors. The reality is that the relativity given to the impact of each of these factors is unknowable in advance. It also depends on the components in terms of missed opportunities and the cost of in appropriate actions because of mistakes, and these components will vary between different organisational structures.

Dynamic resources of the business

The fact that organisational structures have limitations cannot be the whole story. Some businesses are able to not only able to respond to uncertainty and thrive but are able to parlay their position into new opportunities. The proposition presented here is that business continuity requires the development capabilities to do this. This capabilities consists of the knowhow, systems and processes to create, manage and maintain a portfolio of salient strategic options. Salient strategic options are developed for all the sources of uncertainty in the contributors to business value covered in plans and budgets.

The operation of this capability is observed in the business's ability to preserve its vitality and value by regularly realigning the business angle (with the appropriate production process including organisational structure to execute it) to changes in market context. These decisions reset the revenue and cost structure of the business. To provide this vitality, the nature of the capacity to respond will change with the lapse of time.

Choice of activity type and business lifecycle

Expected lifespan of a business influences the choice of business angle

Activity type provides the way to exploit an opportunity given the objectives of and constraints on the business and its owners, and the market context. Both the expected lifecycle of the opportunity and the planned lifetime of the business modify the choice of activity type.

Businesses can be designed with a planned end, where the business is wound-up, determined by the occurrence of an event or at a designated period of time.

Businesses with an expectation of an ongoing lifespan face a three stage lifecycle. The early stage characterised by market share instability, when there are many participants, a mature state where market share is stable and concentrated, and mid-lifecycle which can vary from an initial increase in the number of participants, before the reduction starts in the mature stage of the lifecycle, to a gradual reduction in the number of participants over the entire lifecycle. The lifespans of businesses operating in spontaneous industries and established at short lead-time to take advantage of a speculative opportunity are transient.

The sale or liquidation of a business, which can occur at any point in time, provides strategic options in the form of an off-ramp for owners, and resources, including core competencies, can be redeployed to other business angles.

Expected lifespan and choice of activity type

Businesses designed with an end-of-life have an activity type appropriate to that objective. These businesses focus on a single opportunity, and are managed as a project with a specified whole-of-life business plan. Much of the work to develop the business angle is completed as part of the business activities of other businesses, and is fashioned to exploit a specific market opportunity. For example, a building construction business and a finance business could collaborate on a speculative construction project, by establishing a joint venture. Each of the collaborators would contribute capabilities to the joint venture company from the parent businesses.

Businesses change activity types over the lifecycle of an industry. In the early stage of an industry new businesses use activity types that enable the development of essential core competencies, and buying in of other capacities and other inputs on contract. Mid-lifecycle businesses focus on activity types which maintain and enhance core competencies derived from underlying economies, and adopt activity types appropriate for this purpose. In the mature stage where the industry undergoes consolidation, businesses under stress once again focus on activity types making best use of essential core competencies.

An activity type consisting of only essential core competencies is used by ventures with highly uncertain lifespan such as those established at short notice to take advantage of speculative opportunities and involved in a spontaneous industry.

Summary

An estimate of the lifespan of a business is required to calculate its FCF value. In some settings there is a high degree of uncertainty of the expected lifespan. This may be because the opportunity is speculative or under threat of a significant event which calls into question its continuity. While some businesses are designed to have a limited lifespan to be liquidated on the occurrence of a specified event or point in time, most businesses are managed as an on-going concern. The lifespan of these businesses is related to the investment in strategic options to provide the capacity to respond to changes in market context.

The choice of activity type provides a way to match the objectives, constraints and planned lifespan of the venture, the nature of the business opportunity and its expected lifecycle, and market context. These factors change over time, and consequently the activity types used by a business change over its lifespan.

For businesses operated as going concerns, in the early stage of an industry lifecycle new businesses use activity types that develop essential core competencies. Mid-lifecycle, these businesses focus on activity types that maintain and enhance core competencies derived from underlying economies. In the mature stage of the lifecycle businesses are subject to consolidation, and under stress, focus on activity types that make best use of essential core competencies. Businesses with a defined lifespan, or established at short lead-time to take advantage of a speculative opportunity, or involved in a spontaneous industry, also use activity types consisting of only essential core competencies.

Selected literature review

Early origin of idea

The systematic assessment of risk goes back to mid eighteen century Scotland with the establishment of the Scottish Ministers' Widows' Fund in 1743. Prior to this, risk mitigation actions were priced or had resources applied to realising an outcome as if it were a wager on the occurrence or non-occurrence of an outcome – in other words a subjective bet. The Scottish Ministers' Widows' Fund applied statistical analysis to assess the cost of risk as the likely occurrence of specific life events.

Key influences on the work

An eclectic range of thinking has contributed to these ideas on lifecycle management. These include the discussion of ambiguity by *Complexity, Risk and Financial Markets* by Peters published by John Wiley & Sons in 1999, and the economic implications of uncertainty by O'Driscoll and Rizzo *The Economics of Time and Ignorance: With a New Introduction,* a 1985 publication by Routledge Foundations of the Market Economy.

Jenson and Meckling in a 1995 paper in the *Journal of Applied Corporate Finance* titled 'Specific and general knowledge, and organisational structure' introduce issues of knowledge in organisations, and the devices organisations use to align the interest of knowledge holders with the interests of the organisation.

TEN
Continuous learning to make the most of scarce resources and speculation

Introduction

A central theme in the calculus of seizing a business opportunity takes in expected gains from scarce resources and speculation. In the search for business opportunities businesspeople seek to take advantage of conditions that gives rise to a perceived opportunity for profit in each of the contributors of value. Investment is the consequence of there being businesspeople who judge this an acceptable expected profit, and who are prepared to commit resources to pursuit it. Market context is one of many factors that give rise to the perception that a business opportunity exists or does not exist, other factors being a zeitgeist positively disposed towards investment, and serendipitous openings that present themselves to enter a market.

This, the final chapter, addresses the application of the business angle approach, described in the book, to business development. Following this introduction, there is a synopsis of the conditions that determine and modify business angles. The information to assess the applicability of a business angle is then summarised. This is followed by a discussion of the application of this approach to business planning and budgeting. An outline of some applications to which the business angle approach provides insight is then presented. The final section examines some interpretations of the business angle approach.

Conditions that determine and modify the business angle

The design of the business angle is important to the creation of valuable businesses. Perceived business opportunities stem from expectations to profit. A perceived business opportunity is transformed into an actual business proposition through the choice of the activity type to be implemented to form a business angle. Activity type is intrinsically linked to market context as it aligns business objectives and constraints with conditions found in the market. Quite different types of activities can be employed to form a business angle.

Business angles are determined and modified by a number of factors.

- Market context constrains the range of feasible activity types available to exploit an opportunity. High quantity of demand, market growth rate and volatility in a market provide the conditions of a high range of feasible activity types and vice versa.

- In times of high asset price speculation some feasible business angles consist of more assets than at other times, as the FCF value calculation includes expected increase in asset values as income. Generalising this example to other situations, time and ignorance change the context by increasing the uncertainty and the occasions for speculation. Both factors constrain the range of feasible activity types available to exploit an opportunity, the capabilities used and the assets invested in.

- The removal of shared transaction costs leads to a fragmentation of value networks and the more widespread use of outsourcing adopting the assign method. Where this is associated with positive feedback effects new business opportunities in the form of MSP+s are created. With strong positive feedback effects stimulated, few providers will dominate the market. As a secondary effect, the removal of friction between transacting businesses increases demand as new market segments are opened up. A consequence of this is that items that previously had little monetary value, such as second-hand items through an auction website, now form important trading sectors in which people make their living. The removal of shared transaction costs results in the greater use of activity types based on the assign method, as well as new business opportunities in the value network.

- To accommodate turbulent markets, businesses employ activity types that require least ownership of assets, investing only in essential core competencies and contracting for other capabilities by using the assign method of acquisition.

- Activity types used by a business change over the lifecycle of the industry. In the early stage of an industry new businesses use activity types that develop essential core competencies. Mid-lifecycle businesses focus on activity types that maintain and enhance core competencies derived from underlying economies. The mature stage of the lifecycle businesses are subject to consolidation and are under stress, and concentrate on activity types that make best use of essential core competencies.

That there is a range of quite different activity types available from which to design a business angle is exploited by businesses. Business angles are determined and modified by:

- The desired capital and risk profile to generate an acceptable return to meet the business objectives.

- The strategy adopted to compete in a market. Different activity types are associated with each market positioning strategy, as well as different knowhow, systems and processes.

- The number of different element markets the business operates in. Businesses operate simultaneously in a number of different markets, each of which contributes new opportunities for profit. The number of element markets in which a business operates increases the breadth of core competencies. Profits can be earned from different ways of participating in each of the element markets that contribute value to the business, and consequently the composition of a business's capabilities varies between businesses operating in the same position in a value network.

- Businesses parlay scarce resources along different development paths which commonly result in the need to develop new competencies, and in some settings, new activity types are adopted.

- The order of market play adopted to exploit an opportunity. For example, the apparent stability of markets that result from the success of certain business angles, in fact changes the market, and creates other opportunities, which can then be exploited using quite different activity types. Each order of market play calls for appropriate activity types to create the business angle.

- Whether a venture has a defined lifespan, or is established at short lead-time to take advantage of a speculative opportunity, or is involved in a spontaneous industry. An activity type consisting of only essential core competencies is used by these types of ventures.

Information discovery for the selection of a business angle

Place the high level measure of competitive advantage into context

The information on market context is required to assess the applicability of a business angle. The data collected from the market research to compile a value network map provides information on the stages in the value network, the participants and their relative market shares at each stage in the value network, and changes in the shape of and participants in the value network over time. Information on the participants and the markets can be expanded with access to financial data from businesses. Access to financial data from enough businesses can be used to provide estimates of: the size of demand; market growth rate; the share of value added captured by a business; expectations over the length of time this continues for; and the rate of change in the redistribution of value added between participants in the value network. Information on businesses that are privately held or complex organisations with many product lines may be unavailable, and the only information that can be collected is on market share and competitive behaviour, and product price and benefit. Nonetheless, this information is useful in inferring product positioning strategies being used by the participants.

Where financial data is unavailable on the key competitors at a stage in the value network, an estimate of the ordering of size of competitive advantage may be imputed by the rate of change in market share. The assumption is that businesses with the highest rate of market share growth (in the absence of constraints) have the highest level of competitive advantage. By inference, in stable markets, with no significant change in market share, the size of competitive advantage might be indicated by market share. But this inference needs to be treated with caution, for example, because a business stays in the market as long as it has the resources to do so. The timing of when it exits may depend on other considerations, such as contractual commitments. Once the decision has been made to exit, the timing may be determined by how losses to the owners are minimised.

The following sections discuss the information on a business's relative competitive position that can be extracted from financial data.

Utilising resources efficiently to share in the available value added

A business's value is determined by its ability to capture value added by realising a perceived business opportunity through sales. Scarce resources become more valuable as their scarcity increases, because of their ability to capture a greater share of the value added. An appropriate comparative performance measure, of the productivity of resources utilised to generate sales for established businesses, is net profit margin, which is profit to sales revenue ($\frac{profit}{sales}$), compared to the best performing competitors.

Using financial data as a high level measure of competitive advantage

FCF value standardised against expected future sales ($\frac{FCF\,value}{expected\,future\,sales}$) is the measure of business performance in gaining competitive advantage because it is based on future earning ability. Where this ratio is higher than that for competitors the business has gained competitive advantage over them. Its usefulness in understanding comparative competitive advantage can be shown by using a simple financial model. The competitive advantage of a business with stable and constant expected growth in competitive advantage is estimated with the following simple model:

$$\frac{FCF\,value}{expected\,future\,sales} = \frac{profit}{sales} \times \frac{1+growth\,rate}{discount\,rate - growth\,rate}$$

Expressed using cash flow items for a business this is:

$$\frac{FCF\,value}{expected\,future\,sales} = \frac{(sales - CoGS - M\&S - B\&A - ME)(1 - tax\,rate)}{sales} \times \frac{1+growth\,rate}{discount\,rate - growth\,rate}$$

The abbreviations stand for: cost of goods sold (CoGS); marketing and sales expenditure (M&S), which are the delivery method costs; input buying and administration expenses (B&A), which are the acquisition method costs; and expenditure to maintain the current operating capability (ME).

The expected rate of growth (which, under the assumptions made in this simple model, is less than the discount rate) is dependent on the investment and effectiveness to which resources are used to produce an increase in competitive advantage. The factor *effectiveness in delivering future results* is specific to each business and is determined by the skills and drive of the people involved; the core competencies in business development and other resources available to the business, and the knowhow, systems, processes and organisational structure used for this. *Investment in future earnings* is the expected expenditure on R&D; the increased investment in working capital from the increase in inventories and accounts receivable, less the increase in accounts payable (ΔWC); and expenditure to increase the operating capability (CE). As a formula, the expected rate of growth is:

growth rate = effectiveness in delivering future results × future expenditure on: (R&D + ΔWC + CE)

Incorporating the growth rate into the equation for FCF value standardised to the expected level of future sales, and simplifying and rearranging the equation, it is written as:

$$FCF\,value = expected\,future\,sales \times \frac{profit}{sales} \times \frac{1+effectiveness\,in\,delivering\,future\,results \times investments\,in\,future\,earnings}{discount\,rate - effectiveness\,in\,delivering\,results \times investments\,in\,future\,earnings}$$

The FCF value resolves into four parts: (1) sales - businesses need to make sales to be valuable; (2) the competitive advantage of the production process, which is the productivity of resources utilised to generate sales; (3) the effectiveness of the investment - that is, the capability to manage a portfolio of salient options that provide business continuity; and (4) the investment in future earnings. Under this model, the discount rate is an economy wide variable not under the control of the business.

While it is inevitable that investment needs to be made for businesses to provide the capacity to increase sales and make a business valuable, the key factor is the knowhow, systems and processes that the business has developed, to achieve a high effectiveness of investment in growth in competitive advantage. Investment to increase sales also needs to be made in product design supported by appropriate pricing to increase product value-for-money.

Effectiveness of investment shows the ability of management to plan for, and implement, operational and assurance knowhow, systems and processes that are able to deliver on business development plans with confidence, in addition to choosing and putting in place an appropriate portfolio of salient strategic options. Here, options are being used effectively to enhance profit, and magnify competitive advantage, in the sense that more competitive advantage is being generated with the available resources.

This analysis, using FCF value to expected future sales as the reference point, begs the question, how good is management's view of the future value of the business? Comparing the FCF value to market value, less the liquid cash holding of the business, can resolve this question ($\frac{FCF\ value}{market\ value - cash}$). The more this ratio is different from one, the greater the divergence between management's and the market's assessment of the business's value. However, this ratio is complex to interpret. Its value is determined by planning conventions and practices, the expected earnings and their riskiness, and market demand for equity. Differences in FCF and market values are due to speculation that derives from the market expectations of earnings and their riskiness, dividend pay-out, and demand for the business's equity – a topic discussed in chapter 2.

Assessing performance from the perspective of the contributors to value

Analysis of financial ratios is suitable for a business level estimation of whether a business, as a whole, possesses scarce resources. High level analysis does not provide insight into the sources of a business's core competencies. Financial ratios are unable to conclude that scarce resources exist, where the business also has highly inefficient capabilities, as the high cost inefficient capabilities will hide the value captured by core competencies. For this, analysis of each of the contributors to value needs to be undertaken.

Assessment of operational performance requires idiosyncratic measures that relate specifically to circumstances confronting the business. These measures cover the initiatives to address critical assumptions underpinning the business opportunity, the performance of the essential core competencies, critical success factors to bring plans to fruition, and key drivers and their impact on cash flows. The inference diagram in Figure 26 shows the relationship between these elements, using as an illustration the launch by a new venture of a new product into a new undeveloped market. The critical assumptions being made in launching this product are that there is untapped demand in the target market, and that users place high value on a product with superior user experience design. The critical assumptions are addressed though effective implementation of operational and marketing activities, and in the building of production processes.

The opportunity depicted is a multi-sided market, involving consumers, merchants and suppliers of capacity; and the proposed multi-sided platform has to deliver value to all three participant groups in the face of the alternatives available to the three groups of users. Four essential core competencies are required for this opportunity: systems and processes development; operational capability; marketing and sales to consumers; and marketing and sales to merchants. Some of the key drivers influencing this are outside the control of the business, such as the alternatives available to users, merchants, and suppliers of capacity; whereas the capabilities utilised, and product pricing, as remuneration to suppliers of capacity, are under the control of the business. Critical success factors for this platform are the ability of the platform provider to continuously learn, and to reflect this in the capability build programme. Operational performance is assessed by idiosyncratic measures of performance (referred to as key performance indicators) relating to the critical assumptions, key drivers, critical success factors, and essential core competencies. Operational performance in turn impacts on financial measures.

This inference diagram shows the variables available from the perspective of one of the five contributors of business opportunities, in this case the perspective is that of the product market. The levers, or key drivers, are the initiatives to improve the FCF value of the business. In the example depicted in Figure 26, the levers to grow usage of the platform are in the form of marketing to the two user groups; marketing to stimulate the signup and use by merchants who sell to consumers through the reach of the platform; and marketing to stimulate signup and use by consumers who buy from those merchants through the platform. The third group of users is the suppliers of capacity to fulfil transactions between the two other groups of users.

Figure 26 *Inference diagram for an MSP+ opportunity consisting of consumers, merchants and suppliers (product market contributor)*

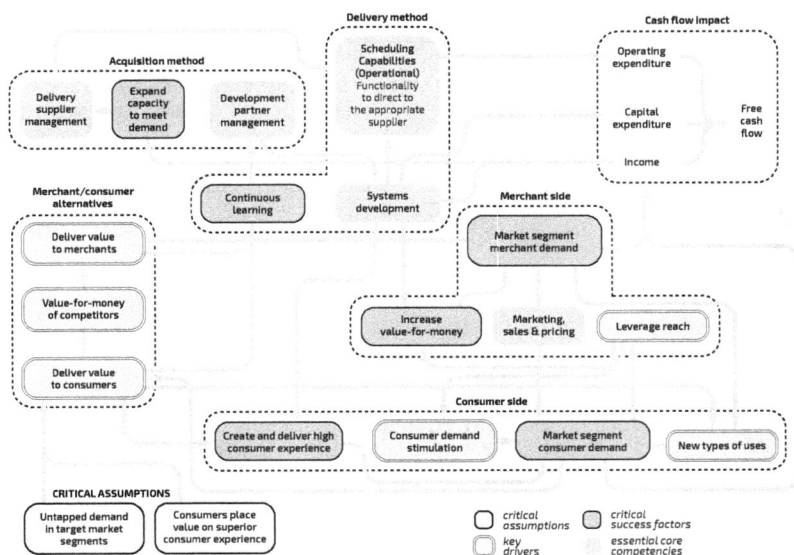

Assessing the contribution of capabilities to business value

Each capability has a place to play in the creation of core competencies, through a relationship with one of the element markets. Establishing the relationship between the capability and contribution to FCF value is achieved by compiling an inference diagram for the perspective to which the capability contributes. The capabilities and relationships described in the inference diagrams for the different contributors to value can be joined together into a more comprehensive inference diagram. By combining inference diagrams in this way the relative contribution of each capability and perspective on the element markets can be assessed.

Analysing a single comprehensive view of the business also addresses any issues of double counting, in which different capabilities claim the same benefits. This technique of combining inference diagrams is especially useful to put costs incurred by a head office in context with operational capabilities and their relative value-for-money contributions assessed. This tackles the issue that head office costs are frequently treated as an overhead and that their contribution to the value of a business is opaque. The capabilities of a head office add value by participating in one or more of the contributors to business value. Head office capabilities should also strive to be scarce resources.

Financial simulation models are used to develop an understanding of the impact of the items selected for inclusion in the inference map on value. Typical issues that are explored with the aid of these models are:

- The size of the potential market and conditions to stimulate rapid growth in sales.
- The strength of the value propositions that will be meaningful to buyers in order to bring about changes in their behaviour to buy the product.
- The degree of innovation required to outdo competition in gaining a share of the available value added.
- The core competencies that will need to be invested in and what will be required of them to address to critical assumptions underpinning the business proposition.
- The key factors that will enable the business to increase market value and attract investors and whether mechanisms are in place to manage them.
- The skills and organisational characteristics required to execute the business plan within the unfolding market context.
- The comparative advantages of different production processes and organisational structures.

Knowing the sensitivity of these items and the implementation tasks that they involve, an implementation plan can be developed that ranks implementation tasks and the commitment of resources by their contribution to creating value.

Business plans and information discovery

The roles of business planning

Implicit in a business plan is a particular view of commerce. When businesspeople promoting a new venture sound out potential financiers for funding they are asked to supply a business plan. In some cases financiers provide a template for the business plan, or recommend specific business planning software be used to present the information. Underpinning many of these popular planning templates and software is the widely held view that business is a causal chain of relationships joining profit, to customers, through products, and the production process (mainly understood in terms of the organisational architecture and staffing levels), and ultimately then to the investment to be made in the venture. This simple relationship between a business idea, presenting it in a business plan and the investment required embodies the return on investment (ROI) approach to business. Deviations from this linear arrow joining investment to profit are allowed for in the form of risks, which are mitigated by further investment. Even in the management of risk, organisational structure is treated as incidental. The processes used by corporations, for the approval of funding for new business initiatives, are no different in their philosophy.

The ROI approach is a financiers' point of view (which is one of the five element markets) and focuses management's actions on generating returns using past investment as the reference point. In contrast, the behaviours expected of new ventures is to deliver on a vision rooted in a perceived opportunity, based on an intimate and insightful understanding of the relevant markets, production process, the resources available (including the drive and experience of the people involved) and constraints on the venture. The attitude to risk can be used to illustrate the different points of view. Various methods are used to gauge, and mitigate, the impact of risk (as narrowly defined) drawing on historical data and knowledge available to the business at the time. Commonly used risk management techniques underestimate the premium for uncertainty because it is difficult to take into account using these techniques. The implication from this is that the premium for uncertainty is different from the assessment of the cost of risks in an ROI approach to business, by some unknown and unknowable amount. Uncertainty takes a more expansive view of its actual impact on business, and the mitigants to be used, than risk does. This is important because it could impact on the choice of business angle selected.

Delivering a vision founded in a perceived opportunity recognises that: speculation in each of the several element markets in which a business operates contributes to profit; uncertainty and option premiums are an integral component of the profit calculation; and value is attributed to the creation of scarce resources. Scarce resources created through economies, in any of the contributors of value, are the embodiment of competitive advantage a business gains. The premiums for uncertainty and options give recognition to the reality that actual profit varies from expected profit because of deviations from expected revenues and cost, and these variations are attributed to uncertainty. While uncertainty is a cost of business it is also a potential contributor to profit though the return from speculation. Uncertainty is a reality that impacts on profitability, and can result in the loss of capital investment. As with many other aspects of business, the magnitude of these costs and benefits is unknown in advance, even though its key drivers may be known. One reason for this is that the net impact of actions to respond to the key drivers of value, and any mitigating actions may not be able to be anticipated with precision beforehand. All that may be said in advance is that the more a business is able to call on, and make use of, existing scarce resources (which include knowhow, systems and processes), the more likely the business is able to address the premium for uncertainty. A high number of resources (brand, core competencies, and the reach and content of an existing MSP+), being utilised to realise a business opportunity, provides one measure of the ability to mitigate uncertainty and meet business plans.

Despite limitations in the way that business plans are applied, they have important roles: as a communications device to unify and focus the people involved in the venture; in revealing the bias of management towards the future earning ability of a business; as a basis for continuous learning in responding to changes in market context; and in signalling the business's competitive strategy to other participants in a value network. The business plan plays a central role in illuminating management's attitude to uncertainty and option premiums. Decisions embodied in the business plan are by necessity ultimately subjective. This is because much of the information that would be useful to formulate plans is unobservable, the available data is ambiguous, or it is unknowable in advance. Other participants are in a similar position of having deficiencies in the information they would like, and each has a different stock of information and ability to make use of it.

Business plans in continuous learning

The business plan is the mechanism whereby all the available knowledge within the business is marshalled to best apply the resources to exploit the perceived business opportunity. The business plan is a point of reference explaining how a business angle is to be executed, the resources available, the selected business model, share of value added available, and targets and outcomes to be achieved. Variations from plan are used to develop questions, and acquire new information, in order to support a continuous learning process, and to refine the business development path. This practice of using the difference between projected position and the actual outturn to uncover new knowledge can be applied to all areas where the business needs new information.

Continuous learning practices are both a way to acquire new information and to develop new capabilities. New knowledge gained is reapplied to refine the way in which resources are applied to best advantage. The process of continuous learning also provides information to assess the benefits from investment in uncertainty and option premiums.

It also has to be recognised that through its actions in executing its business plan, a business signals its strategic intent to competitors. The implication of this is that observing the decisions made by competitors can be used to gain insight into the strategies being implemented.

These roles of business plans in information discovery are a contrast from the use of business plans as a method of management surveillance. The mantra of that use is that there is a causal relationship between planning and success, which is an anathema to an approach that explicitly gives recognition to the reality of the need to invest in risk mitigants and a capacity to respond. The application of resources to continuously learn, and to incorporate this new knowledge into refined plans, is a constituent of the cost of business.

An example of the use of business planning in information discovery that is used in developing a new venture starts with the process of setting down the perceived opportunity, what is wanted from it and the price to be paid for it. It goes on to describe the value network and market context. This requires research to assess the dimensions of the market, identify existing suppliers and buyers, and the benefits and value-for-money of competing products. Some of this research may include talking to buyers. From this groundwork the business angles available to exploit the perceived opportunity are identified. This step culminates with the analysis to discover how the feasible business angles could create competitive advantage and therefore value, and the resource requirements. This is the first point at which the proposition can fail in that no feasible business angle is identified.

The next step in this process is to refine the design of the business angle to go to market in order to exploit the perceived opportunity and validate that a valuable proposition exists. The focus is to explore how any deficiency can be remedied by the business angle without losing the advantages, specify a production process, organisational structure, and assess the likelihood of being able to succeed at monetising the opportunity while minimising any capital loss. This requires detailed analysis of the benefits and price of competing products, methods and cost of acquiring customers, the critical success factors, and the critical assumptions being made. Other considerations are the legal form to be used, structure of the balance sheet, recruitment and remuneration etc. At this point a business model has been described and its viability is assessed. This is the second point at which the proposition can fail.

Subsequent steps for a viable business model are to build a prototype which is an experiment to gather more information on viability of the opportunity and stakeholder support. This is the third point at which the validity of the proposition is tested. From here, the minimum viable proposition is built with the necessary set of features, with the objective of discovering the actual interest in the proposition from the market. This is another opportunity to validate the proposition. This is the point at which the decision is made to scale the operation. Each of the review points in this business planning process provides information to refine and reset the business model, the understanding of the business opportunity and how it can be realised.

Application of the business angle approach

Examples of the application to which the business angle approach provides insights are:

1. *Finding new opportunities in mature markets.* Opportunities can be found in any of the five orders of market play. The first order involves laying claim to a share of the available value added in the value network. The second order covers opportunities from changing the value network. The third order entails gaining a share of the flow of money from re-pricing assets. Fourth order opportunities are associated with fads and bubbles, and the fifth order accounts for the actions of those who exploit situations where trustworthiness cannot be easily established.

2. *Formulating a business model for new business ventures.* A new venture gives effect to exploiting a perceived opportunity. Key considerations in developing the business model are: 'finding the money' associated with the opportunity by unearthing a place in the market; and selecting an activity type that matches the constraints imposed by capital, risk bearing, return expectations and resources. Sixteen sentinel activity types provide the means to create a business angle to take advantage of an opportunity.

3. *Parlaying core competencies.* Where existing businesses undertake investment in new business ventures, a common concern is how to leverage existing core competencies into new opportunities. Five paths can be followed to do this. The most commonly used path is vertical and horizontal integration, Path 1.

Path 2 involves building on strong cross-group effects associated with the parent business angle to form a multi-sided market. Path 3 takes advantage of economies associated with brand, whereas Path 4 uses available scarce resources to develop business angles within a new order of market play. Realising improved market value in financial and asset markets through financial engineering is Path 5.

4. *Exploring business investment strategy for MSP+ businesses* based on considerations of the extent to which: existing resources can be leveraged; the existing multi-sided platform can be enhanced, grown and expanded; and core competencies strengthened and new ones created. The investment strategy is to exploit the MSP+ by (1) driving more value out of it, or (2) deepening its value; (3) broadening its opportunity; (4) exploiting brand; and (5) portfolio diversification.

Underpinning these considerations is the proposition that the more scarce resources exploited by a business angle, the lower the expected premium for uncertainty. Conversely, the premium for uncertainty increases as fewer scarce resources are employed. Investment in diversification is ascribed a high uncertainty premium but is still required to contribute to the development of new core competencies. This favours investment of resources closely aligned to the core business at the time. This bias is brought about by selecting in favour of opportunities that are: consistent with the brand; associated with MSPs, especially those that leverage existing platforms; and use existing core competencies. Opportunities that require resources to create and enhance existing core competencies have the strongest chances of succeeding.

5. *Defining an MSP+ opportunity.* Multi-sided market opportunities are found in value networks that enable parties to transact directly with one another over an MSP. Transacting over the platform is at lower shared transaction cost than any other way. This experience has to provide better value-for-money than that achievable through alternatives and is derived from the removal of significant shared transaction costs. The other key feature, for those opportunities with positive cross-group effects, is being able to stimulate cross-group effects between the different user groups such that it increases the attractiveness to other user groups to also join the platform.

6. *Investigating spontaneous industry opportunities.* In formulating business development polices to support idiosyncratic conditions, such as those related to specific institutional conditions, natural resources, talents and opportunities faced by one or a few individuals in a location, the choice of activity type is crucial. The 16 sentinel activity types provide the means to generate profit from short-lived opportunities.

7. *Restructuring in response to changes in market context.* Businesses facing major changes in market context, such as competition from a market disrupting product, respond by reassessing their business model. Unlike new ventures with limited resources to leverage, an existing business presented with restructuring, faces the challenge of shedding a bias towards legacy in evaluating the reality of the emerging market context. Considerations incorporated into the business model development process are: the emerging contributors of value; value proposition; core competencies (which derive from future profits) and other resources, and the activity type in use.

8. *Evaluating competitive positioning strategies and pricing.* For a business to find a profitable place in a market a business adopts one of five positioning

strategies which derive from: cost advantage, where the business has a low average cost structure compared to competitors (Position 1); local advantage, where the lower cost to a supplier of reaching local buyers is exploited (Position 2); extemporaneous advantage, stemming from conditions where buyers are willing to pay a premium because of a product's availability at the right time and place (Position 3); segmentation advantage, where the attributes of the product are changed so as to provide a targeted sub-group of buyers with better value-for-money than competing products (Position 4); and transaction cost advantage, gained from removing shared transaction costs from parties wishing to transact with one another (Position 5). These positioning strategies are one of the factors determining pricing policy.

9. *Elucidating the value contributed by head offices and other capabilities.*
It is proposed that all capabilities contribute to business profit by operating in one or more of the five contributors of value related to the different element markets in which the business operates. Head office capabilities, as with all other capabilities in the business, potentially contribute value to the business where the line of sight between the contribution of the capability and the value it adds, is transparent. Depending on the business's circumstances, head office capabilities can contribute to any or all of the five contributors of value. In summary, businesses create FCF value by providing buyers with products of greater value-for-money than available from alternatives (Contributor 1). FCF value is also created by selecting a set of inputs to support a highly productive production process, and the economical purchase of those inputs (Contributor 2), and, by operating a high productivity production process to deliver planned outputs (Contributor 3). FCF value is improved by the use of risk mitigants and strategic options (Contributor 4), and business value is enhanced by financial management to make best use of the available resources (Contributor 5).

Concluding remarks

At a benign level the drive of business is the expectation of profits from the commitment of resources to perceived business opportunities. This is despite constraints on resourcing, and imperfect and incomplete information. These limitations drive the creation of solutions to accommodate them, as well as creating new opportunities to profit from them. The expectation of profit relies on hope, and the optimism to perceive and pursue business opportunities. This is a presumption in the face of ignorance of future outcomes. At a pragmatic level business decisions are driven for most businesspeople by the requirement to earn a living for those involved in the venture. For some, it is also the chance to enter a lottery with the prospect of earning a fortune.

Dynamism in business is driven by resource-use decisions, based on the expectation of realising a profit. The winners in exploiting any particular business opportunity can 'take all'. This is because the exercise of economic power to capture value added is widespread. But short of gaining control of law-making, these winners cannot arrest the emergence of new opportunities and businesspeople to exploit them to the detriment of incumbents. Other facets of human behaviour that impact on economic decisions, such as societal values, and personal ethics, are clearly relevant, as is the fact that the burden of systemic business failures is paid by unsecured creditors, and ultimately by society. Society pays through the loss of jobs and asset values, and tax payers having to fund government interventions.

Participation in commerce is characterised by: dedication being required from businesspeople; the force of circumstances (aka necessity); lack of knowledge, especially about the future (aka ignorance); aspirations and hope (aka delusion); the inextricable reality of economic forces of unrelenting change and flexing of economic power (aka tyranny); and serendipity (aka luck). These factors can be marshalled, at least for a period of time, by creativity and innovation in the design of the business angle, with the supporting scaffolding of the production process (including the organisational structure). While the creativity drawn on in the making of a successful business is on a par with that of a masterpiece, making profits from business is quite unlike the creation of a great masterpiece. That requires prodigious skill and workmanship. In business there is a large element of luck to making money, similar to winning a lottery against a backdrop of many failures. Because of the pervasiveness and ongoing presence of uncertainty in business it is not always easy to distinguish between the lucky, the highly-skilled, the lucky, highly-skilled and the lucky charlatan. Each will claim the accolades of the hero as a great master of the art and science of business, as will those who have power, however derived and worthy, to capture a share of the money flows.

This is an optimistic view of commerce as a collaborative enterprise, with day-to-day transactions to a large part based on trust, the pricing mechanism from the participation of large numbers of buyers and suppliers of alternatives, and the creative drive to construct successful businesses. The pursuit of business opportunities, and formulation of business angles, is a widespread activity, and not one that is practised successfully only by elite, all-knowing strategists and serial entrepreneurs, who claim to be able to 'divine and design' market disruptive propositions and organisational structures.

Perceived business opportunities are exploited using a range of quite different activity types. Some businesspeople invest directly in assets, while others find ways to be involved through activity types that do not have the same capital requirements or risk characteristics. Taken as a whole, the perceived opportunity can be exploited by a range of quite different types of activity. These different activity types all seek to exploit the same perceived opportunity, and share in the available value added or the money flow. Activity types differ in their net cash flow and risk profile.

Selected literature review

Early origin of idea

The underlying idea of using the available information to formulate the starting proposition, and to use this to learn, is attributed to Thomas Bayes in *An Essay Towards Solving a Problem in the Doctrine of Chances,* published in 1763.

Key influences on the work

Planning, especially in the form of strategic plans, transformation plans, business cases and budgets, is in widespread use in business. They can be applied to various domains, including business, marketing, ICT, people capability and finance. Preparing these corporate documents is widely practiced, and in some cases the development of these documents is a role played by management consultants.

The vast majority of these plans are prepared under the assumption that there is a causal relationship between actions described in the plan to use resources, by assigning responsibility and accountability, and measuring performance and the targeted outcome. A 'get out of jail card' is provided by risk analysis. Larger businesses frequently use in-house developed templates. Needless to say, most of the plans are not realised and conveniently forgotten; only to be over-taken by new sets of plans, supported by new rhetoric, making outlandish claims of the new era, and what will be achieved. Management writers, such as Henry Mintzberg, have pointed out deficiencies in planning - see his 1994 book *The Rise and Fall of Strategic Planning: Reconceiving Roles for Planning, Plans, Planners* published by Free Press.

Measurement approaches to monitor performance to plan are in wide use. As one example, Total Quality Management places emphases on measurement of performance in order to improve quality in production processes. The measures to monitor business plans commonly rely on easily available sources of data. That there are limitations with business performance measurement approaches is known, including how inappropriate measure lead to unintended outcomes. W Edwards Deming, a leading advocate of quality management, considered 'management by use only of visible figures, with little consideration of figures that are unknown or unknowable' to be a management deadly sin (from *Out of the Crisis* a 1986 publication by Massachusetts Institute of Technology).

Much has been written about the benefits of continuous learning. There is also an expansive literature on the application of Bayesian analysis to decision-making. Also informative here, is the work on the philosophy of science.

"...in almost every phase of ... development ... we are under the sway of ... untestable – ideas; ideas which not only determine what problems of explanation we shall choose to attack, but also what kinds of answers we shall consider as fitting or satisfactory or acceptable, and as improvements of, or advances on, earlier answers... [These preconceived ideas and solutions] are only occasionally discussed as such: more often, they are implicit in the theories and in the attitude and judgements of the [decision makers] ..." (Karl Popper's 1956 book *Quantum Theory and the Schism in Physics* published by Rowman and Littlefield in 1982. Text in brackets added by author).

Glossary

Activity type	Activity type of a business is the specific method used to transform acquired inputs into delivered outputs.
Agency costs	Agency costs are a specific type of transaction cost that arises when the interests of the agent are misaligned to those of the principal. These costs include the agent using the principal's resources for their own benefit, the costs such as monitoring, and incentives and sanctions to align the interests of the agent with those of the principal, and the risk the principal faces from non-performance by the agent.
Agent	Agents and principals are the parties to a contractual arrangement in which the principal sets the terms and conditions to be fulfilled by agents.
Aggregate method	Aggregate method providing products by operate capabilities using the knowhow, systems and processes that depend on the law of large numbers and scale-free infrastructure networks.
Application products	Application products extend the use of knowhow, systems and processes to new adjacent workflow processes or value networks by providing additional functionality.
Arbitrage method	Arbitrage method involving the knowhow, systems and processes to identify differences in the price of products and assets that are caused by asymmetries in information and high transaction cost. This method relies on transaction specific knowledge, which can arise from barriers to information, location, time, customer relationships, etc.
Assemble method	Assemble method using knowhow, systems and processes to produce products by exploiting economies of scale and scope. With these types of products decision-making rights to consume or use are transferred to the buyer on sale, if not entirely, then at least for a period of time.
Asset	1. Assets are items with positive value that the business has ownership rights over or control of.
	2. Assets are stocks of benefits and include tangible assets (e.g. land, building, machinery, tools and inventory) and intangible assets (e.g. goodwill, patents, working capital and bank accounts). Assets may not have a market value and are recorded in the Balance Sheet following GAAP.
Assign method	Assign method producing products using knowhow, systems and processes to operate capabilities that gain efficiencies by improving coordination, by ensuring close alignment of the interests between buyer and supplier.
Bandwagon effect	Bandwagon effect is a social network effect that occurs when demand increases with more users, for example, phone networks attract more users as usage increases.
Bargaining power	The ability to dictate the allocation of value added.
Benefit	Benefit is derived from product attributes that can be real, service attributes and include intangible benefits from product meaning, brand association, fashion and bandwagon effects, to name a few.

Boundary of the business	Boundary of the business refers to the scope of the activities undertaken within a business.
Business	Business refers to any entity engaged in exploiting a business angle. In this setting, a business can be a business unit within an existing corporate, a new start-up venture, consortium, joint venture, or a businessperson operating on their own account. A business may or may not be constituted as a legal entity, such as a limited liability company or cooperative society, amongst other forms.
Business angle	A business angle is a perceived opportunity and an activity type to exploit it. This is a bottom up concept in which a businessperson using the limited information available seeks to find a potential source of profit.
Business model	The business model is the way in which the business opportunity is converted into profit. This covers the activity type including its knowhow, systems and processes, organisational structure, product specifications, and target buyers.
Business opportunity	Business opportunity is an intervention in a market to potentially earn profit.
Business proposition	A business proposition is used here to mean a description of a business opportunity with supporting business model to exploit it as documented in business plans and other corporate documents.
Capability	Capability utilise the business's resources through the application of knowhow, systems and processes to perform actions. The capabilities in a business differ in the functions they perform in their contribution to the methods used to acquire inputs and deliver products.
Capital	Capital is the funds provided by lenders and investors. The price of capital from lenders is the interest rate charged. The return to investors is a share of profits such as dividends.
Cluster of businesses	A coalition of businesses in supply/buyer relationships that compete with other clusters in a value network. Clusters can be formal relationships or loose groups, for example based on geographic location.
Cognitive bias	The systematic deviation from logical decision-making is ascribed to cognitive bias. Behaviour scientists have identified a wide variety of these limitations, such as the sunk cost fallacy.
Commodities	Commodities are consumed in production processes. Commodities include resources such as labour effort, electricity, and lease on property, and are recorded in the GAAP Profit and Loss statements as expenses. Commodities are usually purchased using market and bilateral contracts.
Competing alternatives	Buyers have the choice between direct competitors offering similar products to the same market, indirect competitors offering a similar product but to a different market, and substitute products to the same market.
Competitive advantage	Competitive advantage is the value that is attributed to scarce resources and is measured by FCF value. High competitive advantage is associated with high FCF value of scarce resources – which incorporate the ability to generate profits in the future – for the expected sale.

Contractual commitments	Contractual commitments is a catchall category for items that arise from express terms and conditions between the parties to an agreement, sometimes in the form of a legally binding agreement and which are not otherwise classified as commodities and assets. Contractual commitments are intertwined with the business's dealings in all element markets. Importantly contractual claims can create assets as well as liabilities for the business. These contracts can be bilateral or trilateral. GAAP and tax authorities have specific rules for the treatment of some contractual commitments.
Contributors of value	There are five contributors that can improve FCF value. They do this by: improving the value-for-money of products that leads to improved revenue (Contributor 1); improving the selection and purchase of inputs that result in lower input costs (Contributor 2); improving the productivity and effectiveness of the production process to enhance scarce resources (Contributor 3); improving the use of appropriate risk mitigants to ensure that business plans are met, and improving the use of strategic options to extend the on-going profitability of the business(Contributor 4); and improving financial management so that it contributes to the value of the business (Contributor 5).
Core competency	A core competency is a capability or set of capabilities that contributes to the creation of positive FCF value. The competitive advantage businesses enjoy stems from resources created, which are valuable, rare and difficult to imitate. Generally this is because they are derived from accumulated experience and knowledge, and/or investment in organisational wide systems.
Cost of friction	Also called transaction cost.
Critical assumptions	Critical assumptions are known uncertainties about the business model and market context that are required to be true for the planned outturn to be realised.
Critical success factor	The attainment of a state necessary to achieve the planned outcome is a critical success factor.
Cross-group effect	Cross-group effect is the phenomenon in which demand by one group is influenced by demand by another group. This effect is positive, neutral or negative.
Cross-product effect	Cross-product effect occurs where demand for a product is determined by demand for another product. Examples include substitutes and complements. In some cases this increase in demand can have a positive feedback effect and increase demand for the original product. For example, size of product range (content) increases so the demand for all products increases (such as devices on which to play the content).
Demand curve	A demand curve shows the relationship between price and the quantity of a product bought.
Development paths	The various ways in which core competencies are used to create new business angles. There are five development paths whereby core competency leveraging: positioning for new opportunities within a value network (Path 1), leveraging the initial market into a multi-sided market opportunity (Path 2), extending the brand associated with the parent business angle (Path 3), applying scarce resources to different orders of market play (Path 4), and realising through financial engineering improved market value in financial and asset markets (Path 5).

Development strategies	Strategies used to launch initiatives to open up new business angles within a value network: growing market share (Direction A), expansion into allied markets (Direction B), changing the activity type through vertical integration (Direction C), changing the activity type to improve profit in current product markets (Direction A), and expanding into new markets that require investment in new activity types.
Economies	Declining cost economies are positive feedback effects that create value added through lower average costs, increasing barriers to entry or lower transaction costs, and include those derived from size, scale and scope achieved in the operation of knowhow, systems and processes; agency costs, the law of large numbers, scale-free infrastructure networks and density economies; asymmetries in access to information, knowledge, institutional arrangements, and location and time.
Efficient market	An efficient market operates where there are many buyers and sellers who have access to appropriate information to make a rational decision and there are low transaction costs involved.
Element markets	The element markets are the range of different markets in which a business operates, which includes the markets for product, commodity, assets, financial assets and contractual commitments.
Enterprise	Synonym for business.
Essential core competencies	Minimum viable set of capabilities to provide core competencies to profitably implement a business angle.
Exchange products	Exchange products provide a high degree of readiness for use, through for example, custom, standardisation and specification, and transfer decision-making rights to consume or use to the buyer on sale, if not entirely, then at least for a period of time.
Expected profit	Expected profit is the planned for profit based on estimates of income, less costs including the premiums for uncertainty and options.
FCF	Free cash flow – see profit.
FCF value	FCF value is calculated as the net present value of expected future free cash flow.
Feedback effects	Feedback effects refer to the nature of the interrelationship between the attainment of one state (e.g. volume produced) and value of another state (e.g. cost structure). Feedback effects can be supply and demand-side effects and the impact can be positive, negative or neutral. For example, with the production of more output the impact of positive feedback is declining average costs and negative feedback would result in increasing average costs.
Flow of money	Flow of money refers to money transactions that include payments for salaries and wages, products and assets, capital investment, loans and other forms of debt, dividends and interest payments, government transfers and taxes.
Friction	Another term for transaction cost.
GAAP	Generally Accepted Accounting Principles.
ICT	Information and communications technology.
Inference diagram	An inference diagram shows the relationship between initiatives to address critical assumptions underpinning the business opportunity, the performance of the essential core competencies, critical success factors, and key drivers and their impact on cash flow.

Information asymmetries	Information asymmetries refer to situations where one party has better information than others and this causes the parties to behave differently. Information asymmetries arise from constraints on access to data, deficiencies in knowledge, from institutional arrangements, from geographic location, and because of time.
Innovation	Innovations are improvements instigated by a business in any of the five contributors to FCF value.
Inputs	In the setting of the definition of profit, an input is any cash expenditure such as on commodities and assets.
Institutional arrangements	Institutional arrangements cover, for instance, social conventions, the law and agreements.
Interface products	Interface products are associated with the interaction with systems and processes, or channel for delivering exchange products.
Investment	The commitment of assets, including capital, resources, labour (such as in sweat equity) and reputation to a business.
Key drivers	Key drivers are the independent variables that determine an outcome. For example, price is a key driver of sales.
Key performance indicator	A key performance indicator is an idiosyncratic measure which when used with targets shows the attainment of performance towards meeting planned outcomes.
Law of large numbers	The phenomenon where, with more occurrences of an unconnected event, the occurrence of an event lies more closely to the average occurrence of the event.
Legal form	The legal arrangement under which a business is constituted is its legal form, for example as a publicly listed company and limited liability private company.
Market	A market is the institutions, social conventions, infrastructure, and capabilities that facilitate the repeated exchange of products, assets, skills, capital, information and other resources.
Market context	Market context is an umbrella term for the situation that applies to a particular market, including its size, suppliers and buyers, the products, and societal expectations, institutional arrangements cultural norms in which it operates.
Market disruption	A market disruption is a buyer experience that occurs when comparative value-for-money changes rapidly enough to be noteworthy, forcing a re-evaluation of spending patterns.
Market segmentation strategies	Businesses use market positioning strategies to find a place in a market, these positioning strategies are derived from advantages that stem from: cost (Position 1), local (Position 2), extemporaneous (Position 3), segmentation (Position 4), and transaction cost (Position 5).
Market turbulence	The rate of change in the make-up and preferences of customers for a business's products is the market turbulence.
Market value	Market value is the price obtained for a product or asset in a fair sale. When applied to the business it is the market value for the business as a going concern.
Method	Method is a set of capabilities enabling the acquisition of inputs or delivery of outputs.
MSP+	Multi-sided platform with positive cross-group effects.

Multi-sided platform (MSP)	Multi-sided platform enables two or more parties to transact directly with one another. This is done by providing the platform for interchanges between various parties, but not actually taking part in the contractual relationship between the parties.
Net assets	Calculated as the difference between the value of assets and liabilities. Because accounting data is readily available, depreciated book values are used. These accounting values can give a poor approximation of the value under different conditions, such as a going concern.
Net income	Net income is the residual income after meeting all cash outflow commitments (the costs) including the option premium of resources employed over the investment horizon.
Nodes	A node comprises the capabilities to deliver outputs and operates at one stage in the value network delivering products to the next stage. A business consists of one or more nodes.
Opportunity cost	The opportunity cost is the net benefit forgone by pursuing the best alternative course of action.
Option	An option confers the right, but not an obligation, to undertake a certain course of events. A tradeable option contract involves the purchaser of the option paying a fee for the right to buy (called a call option) or sell (this is a put option) a real or financial asset at a specified price. A real option is the right but not the obligation to undertake some real business activity, such as constructing or selling a building. Unlike tradable option contracts, real options, in general, cannot be traded as securities and may not be precisely time bound. The term option is used in two ways:

1. Strategic options which provide the capacity to respond to uncertain events so as to provide on-going continuity for the business.

2. Tactical options that address short term variations due to events such as price fluctuations. |
Option premium	The option premium is the resource allocated to maintain and enhance the on-going income earning ability of the business.
Orders of market play	The ways in which business opportunities are exploited. There are five orders of market play: working within a value network, (Order 1), aiming to reform a value chain and its markets (Order 2), changing the flow of money between the different participants and markets in different value networks (Order 3), fuelling fads and bubbles (Order 4), and exploiting performance ambiguity (Order 5).
Organisational structure	The organisational structure refers to knowledge acquisition, business strategy, organisational architecture and incentive schemes.
Outputs	In the setting of the definition of profit, an output is any cash income, most importantly products. Some outputs are inputs that are resold.
Participants	Participants are involved with a business and in a value network, including buyers, providers, suppliers, competitors and government.
Participation curve	The participation curve shows the operation of cross-group effects, particularly how usage of a platform by one group of users changes with different levels of access to another group of users.
Parties	Parties are particular participants in a transaction that involve contractual claims, such as buyers and their suppliers, and principals and agents. For example, there are parties to a contract and participants in a market.

Perceived benefit	The benefits to the buyer including aspirational benefits in the form of its product meaning, such as its allure within the culture and context in which the product is offered for sale.
Platform	A platform is a highly scalable production process that removes a set of shared transaction costs faced by large groups of users.
Premium for uncertainty	The premium for uncertainty is cost to cope with the unexpected, in order to realise business plans and budgets. The cost consists of risk mitigants and the consequences to flow from the occurrence of uncertain events.
Price elasticity of demand	Price elasticity of demand is a measure of the proportionate change in quantity demanded as a result of a proportionate change in price. In most cases it is less than negative one.
Principal	See explanation for agents.
Product	Product is used as a generic term for items that are exchanged between parties in product markets and have attributes that provide benefits such as service quality.
Product meaning	Product meaning refers to how buyers relate to a product because of connotations associated with its physical, functional, symbolic and cultural attributes.
Product type	Exchange, interface and application products are different product types.
Production process	The production process is the overarching term for the collection of capabilities used by the business. A production process has organisational structure, activity type that uses production technology with appropriate knowhow, systems and processes, resources, and contractual obligations to transform inputs into outputs.
Profit	A business's profit during a period is the net operating profit after tax, less the change in working capital and expenditure required to maintain the operating profit. This definition of profit is also known as free cash flow. An approximation of free cash flow from the financial accounts of a business is EBIT (1 – tax rate) + depreciation and amortization – change in working capital – expenditure to maintain the current operating capability.
Profit margin	A profit margin is the ratio of profit to sales revenue.
Resource	A resource is a source or supply of profit. To illustrate this concept, whereas real estate property is an asset, the flow of benefits it provides (e.g. shelter, prestige) is a resource. The asset can be sold. By letting real estate the resource is sold. Other examples of resources are labour effort and knowhow.
Return from speculation	The return on speculation is the contribution to profit to recognise the gain or loss from changes in product and asset prices, and other inputs from participating in the market.
Return on investment (ROI)	ROI is the gain from an investment less its cost divided by its cost.
Return on marketing investment (ROMI)	Return on marketing investment is calculated as the incremental margin for marketing expenditure divided by marketing expenditure.

Risk	1. The variation from the target value that is anticipated and its consequences assessed. Risk is management's expectation of the variation, but is only one component of uncertainty. Before the event it is impossible to know the degree to which risk is aligned to the uncertainty.
	2. Synonym for uncertainty, connoting exposure to loss which, for example, could result in loss of capital invested.
Scale-free infrastructure network	Scale-free infrastructure network relates to production processes, especially infrastructure networks, which involve high initial fixed cost and diminishing costs, and which follow a power law relationship for the addition of more users.
Scarce resources	Scarce resources are distinguished from other assets by their price being established by their profit earning ability. Scarce resources include core competencies and can include physical assets, financial assets and legal rights.
Simulacra	Simulacra opportunities occur in markets where a product experiences positive notoriety and involves the creation of new products embodying a hyper reality interpretation of the brand attribute surrounding the product.
Social network effect	Contagions that occur between people in a group (which can be buyers, sellers, finance providers, friends). These contagions can be spread by word-of-mouth and the bandwagon effect.
Speculation	Speculation is the act of picking a future price for a product or asset.
Spontaneous industries	Spontaneous industries are short-lived clusters of businesses in a locality centred on a single industry that emerge where conditions are conducive and last for only as long as those conditions persist.
Stage	Value networks are broken in stages by markets. A stage comprises capabilities organised into one or more nodes.
Strategy	A set of directed actions to realise an objective.
Structural changes	Changes to nature and characteristics of the value network together with the wider institutional, commercial and social structures in which a business operates.
Super profit	A business earns super profit when its profit is significantly more than that achievable by competitors and its source is strong bargaining power, high barriers to copying and high value-for-money of its products.
System	1. 1. A network of capabilities and information flows with resultant behaviour responses to external stimuli. In this meaning a business is a system, as is a value network.
	2. The equipment, software, plant, machinery, infrastructure and procedures used in processes following prescribed procedures, which provide the capability and capacity to deliver a business's outputs, for example a computer system.
Transaction cost	The costs incurred in the process of businesses transacting are transaction cost. These include searching, negotiating, changes to be able to use the product, ambiguity in scope of the product being contracted for, monitoring performance, invoicing and payment, maintaining documentation and performance failure.

Uncertainty	Uncertainty is the variation from the target value. Uncertainty ranges from risk (that is, the known unknowns in which the likelihood of events occurring can be assessed); through to acknowledgement of unknown knowns, for example, severe rare events where the potential for occurrence is recognised even though their occurrence may be unknown; and on through to unknowable events. These events can occur in all contributors to business value and cover uncertainty in price, opportunity, input, capability, decision, business value, and regulatory and institutional arrangements.
Value added	Value added is the sum of the surpluses multiplied by the quantity consumed enjoyed by all parties in a value network.
Value controller	A business with high bargaining power that exerts a high degree of control over the allocation of value added in a value network has the ability to dictate, at least for a period of time, the pace of change in the value network.
Value network	Value network is a network of capabilities, usually in more than one business, which culminates in the capacity to deliver products to the final consumer.
Value network map	A value network map is a depiction of the stages in a value network, the participants at each stage as measured by their market share, and the relationship between the participants.
Value proposition	Value proposition is the promise that a product will deliver perceived benefits to the buyer for the price.
Value-for-money	Value-for-money is the surplus from the difference between the perceived benefit to the buyer of a product and its price.
Venture	A business with the connotation of a high speculative component for expected profit.

Index

Acknowledgements

I owe a debt of gratitude to the numerous people who have contributed to the making of this book. There are the people who have, in my capacity as a management consultant, provided opportunities for me to refine the methods which are now presented in this book. Some of the examples presented are drawn from these projects. Then, there are my business colleagues who have also contributed. Discussions with fellow businesspeople have been an important way in which ideas have been expanded. I have learnt from their experiences in creating businesses and dealing with the realities of running a business. Some of this has also made its way into the book.

I would like to thank each and every one for your contributions. Without your support this work would not have been undertaken.

I would also like to thank the following who have contributed directly to the publication process: Linda Bowater, Kerri Du Pont, Lynn Lawrence and Meredith Thatcher.